100

THINGS TO DO IN
CLEVELAND
BEFORE YOU
DIE

Photo Credit: Cody York

100

THINGS TO DO IN
CLEVELAND
BEFORE YOU
DIE

• •

NIKKI DELAMOTTE

REEDY PRESS

Copyright © 2016 by Reedy Press, LLC
Reedy Press
PO Box 5131
St. Louis, MO 63139, USA
www.reedypress.com

Library of Congress Control Number: 2016940398

ISBN: 9781681060538

Design by Jill Halpin
Cover image: Cody York for ThisisCleveland.com

Printed in the United States of America
16 17 18 19 20   5 4 3 2 1

Please note that websites, phone numbers, addresses, and company names are subject to change or cancellation. We did our best to relay the most accurate information available, but due to circumstances beyond our control, please do not hold us liable for misinformation. When exploring new destinations, please do your homework before you go.

Photo Credit: Cody York

CONTENTS

● ●

Music and Entertainment

• •

Sports and Recreation

Culture and History

• •

• •

PREFACE

Cleveland is a city ever-evolving. By the time you've cracked the spine of this book, an artist will put the final touches on a gallery show in 78th Street Studios, a musician will send an album to Gotta Groove Records for pressing, and someone who just moved to Cleveland will look out over the Tower City observation deck at the land of the new place they call "home."

This is the place people come to make their dreams a reality. *100 Things to Do in Cleveland Before You Die* highlights the rewards of the gritty resilience of those who are building the city with their own two hands. Ask any Clevelander—especially the ones tirelessly tailgating in the Muni Lot before every Cleveland Browns game—and they'll tell you that we're tough, but we have heart. Superman was born here thanks to two kids in Glenville, after all.

Our culture is as rich as our land along Lake Erie. Walk down the brick-lined road of East 4th Street and you'll find James Beard Award-winning chefs serving the same produce we get from our wealth of farmers's markets and historic haven West Side Market. In Old World neighborhoods like Tremont, we hold our beloved ethnic cuisines with the same level of devotion as we do chic celebrity chef restaurants a block away. No one forgets their first time at Sokolowski's University Inn.

The beauty of our appreciation for old and new should come as no surprise. This is, of course, the rock and roll capital of the world. We walk through walls filled with history at the Rock & Roll Hall of Fame and Museum, but we also rally around our concert clubs, our local vinyl shrines, and Lottery League. More about that extravaganza later.

To limit this book to 100 things to do and see seems impossible—because it absolutely is. We suggest you begin in the Flats by way of the Towpath Trail or Midwest Railway open house. Read the true stories of the city written on walls and storefronts through the street art of Cleveland SGS.

Hit the pavement with Harness Cycle to run the bridges. As you stand under the Guardians of Transportation and look out over the Cleveland skyline, you'll know you've only just begun. And as we said, by the time you've finished with this, there will be at least one hundred more things just sprouting up in Cleveland to add to your list.

So stroll through the sprawling Cleveland Cultural Gardens, dance through the streets to the tune of Cleveland-style polka on Dyngus Day, and absorb the challenging works of Cleveland Public Theatre and Karamu House. Just don't forget to work up an appetite at Superelectric Pinball Parlor before you fill up on hot dogs topped with Froot Loops at Happy Dog. The world-renowned Cleveland Orchestra will be there waiting to serenade you.

It's what we call a warm Cleveland welcome, and you'll find it here every day.

Photo Credit: Frank Lanza

FOOD AND DRINK

STAND IN LINE
FOR A SLYMAN'S SANDWICH

Everyone remembers their first Slyman's experience. Given the price tag of one sandwich, at first you will be surprised by the long line of die-hard fans waiting to get into this modest, unpretentious deli. You've heard it's the closest thing to a New York-style deli and you're eager to know whether you should believe all the hype. But then you get your plate, which is anything *but* modest. Piled a mile high is the colossal corned beef sandwich that you've heard so much about—thinly sliced, juicy cuts stuffed between two fragrant slices of rye bread. Suddenly you know why everyone's packed into this no-frills shop. Under different circumstances, servers might feel flustered by the crowds. Not at Slyman's; they're used to this. They just swing by and ask, "Need a refill?"

3106 St. Clair Ave. NE, Cleveland
216-621-3760, slymans.com

GET A BIRD'S-EYE VIEW
OF THE WEST SIDE MARKET

Long before West 25th was the bustling, brewery-filled district it is today, the West Side Market became a vibrant cornerstone of Ohio City when it was built in 1912. Today, the city's oldest public market is buzzing with local businesses and plenty of Old World charm.

Make a beeline to Frank's Bratwurst, which has been serving up the meaty Cleveland favorite since 1970. Then go from stand to stand nibbling on the smorgasbord of offerings, from farm-fresh produce to an ethnic melting pot of freshly made shepherd's pie, gyros, crepes, and falafel.

To fully appreciate the grand spectacle, grab your food and ascend to the balcony overlooking the entire indoor market by following the staircase near the West 25th Street entrance. This respite from the swelling crowds isn't simply a photo-worthy view, but a chance to take in everything that's been built over the last century.

1979 W 25th St., Cleveland
216-664-3387, westsidemarket.org

BE A CHEF FOR THE DAY
AT CULINARY VEGETABLE INSTITUTE

Chefs are undoubtedly the new rock stars, whether we're talking internationally known celebrity chef Michael Symon of Food Network fame or the friendly face at your neighborhood diner. The Culinary Vegetable Institute allows that fantasy to run wild with their Chef for a Day program, where you wear the hat and apron and create a locally-sourced dinner for guests under the direction of their expert chefs. If you're not ready to be the next Doug Katz or Karen Small, a visit to CVI's one-hundred-acre state-of-the-art facility is still enticing on its own. Chefs from around the world travel to CVI to host dinners, their own chefs have developed a farm-fresh meal series, and cooking classes abound. You can also visit the partnering Chef's Garden farm for a true earth-to-table experience.

12304 Mudbrook Rd., Milan
419-499-7500, culinaryvegetableinstitute.com

RELIVE HOUGH CAKE MEMORIES
AT ARCHIE'S HOUGH BAKERY

Just say the words "daffodil cake" to any Northeast Ohioan native and you're likely to get a nostalgic recollection of the long lines at Hough Bakeries for Easter sweets. Weddings, graduation parties, special occasions? Hough's white cake with that sweet frosting was there. Once one of the largest bakery operations in Cleveland, Hough has since closed its doors after ninety-year-run of providing treats for the Cleveland area that began in 1903. But Hough's skilled employees are still around and the result is Archie's Hough Bakery, the last shop using Hough recipes. Former head baker Archie Garner opened his storefront bake shop and keeps the classic recipes alive. Those recipes are still secret, of course, but it's a taste that brings back a flood of memories for anyone who ever longed for just one more slice.

14906 Lakeshore Blvd., Cleveland, 216-481-4188

EAT YOUR WAY
THROUGH EAST 4TH STREET

The brick-lined road and strings of lights dangling between buildings may add a magical touch to what's become the most lively street in the city and a culinary wonderland. Food Network Iron Chef Michael Symon's restaurants Lola and Mabel's BBQ are shining gems, James Beard Award-winning chef Johnathon Sawyer's The Greenhouse Tavern is a farm-to-table masterpiece, and restaurateur Zack Bruell's Chinato serves Italian with elegance.

But it's not just a foodie haven. Knock back bowling pins and martinis at the sleek Corner Alley and see the best regional and national comedians at Pickwick and Frolic comedy club. Wear your city pride on your sleeve by picking up new gear at Cleveland Clothing Company.

2015 E 4th St., Suite 220, Cleveland
216-589-1111, east4thstreet.com

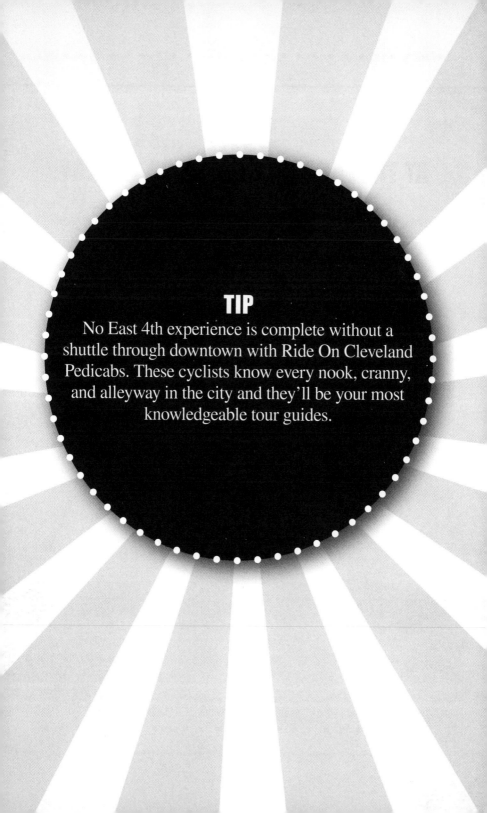

TIP

No East 4th experience is complete without a shuttle through downtown with Ride On Cleveland Pedicabs. These cyclists know every nook, cranny, and alleyway in the city and they'll be your most knowledgeable tour guides.

STAY
AT THE LAKEHOUSE INN AND WINERY

There are dozens of reasons to visit Northeast Ohio's wine country (and many of them come in a glass, extra dry). But you may not want to step foot outside the Lakehouse Inn, especially when there are wine tastings right on site. You will really enjoy dining farm-to-table at the inn's restaurant, Crosswinds Grille. But that shouldn't stop you from testing out everything the region has to offer with destinations like M Cellars and Rennick Meat Market. And while you are at it, plan to spend at least a day at Geneva-on-the-Lake's strip for deep-fried fair food, Ferris wheel rides, and carnival games. We promise that Lakehouse's gourmet cuisine and R&R will all still be there when you get back.

5653 Lake Rd. E, Geneva
440-466-8668, thelakehouseinn.com

ADD FROOT LOOPS TO YOUR HOT DOG
AT THE HAPPY DOG

When it comes to the fifty-two toppings you can pile on top of your hot dog at the Happy Dog, we recommend the alien pickle relish. Or SpaghettiOs. Or Froot Loops. Or all three together. Let's face it, the possibilities are endless, especially when the franks are cheap and come in beefy or vegan varieties.

While nomming on a side of tater tots, you're likely to see the stage filled with polka players, soul-spinning DJs, garage rock bands, or members of the Cleveland Orchestra depending on the night.

Though this corner joint has long been the beloved hot dog epicenter of Gordon Square, they recently took their dogs to the east side to set up a second location in the former space of The Euclid Tavern.

5801 Detroit Ave., Cleveland
216-651-9474, happydogcleveland.com

11625 Euclid Ave., Cleveland
216-231-5400, happydogcleveland.com

BE FRENCH FOR A DAY
AT COQUETTE PATISSERIE

Escape to Paris in this quaint little nook in the Uptown neighborhood. French pastries and macarons are specialties within these close quarters, but the small size of the shop only adds to the charm of stopping in for a hot tea or French press coffee in the morning or the romance of cozying up with a special someone on date night.

The elegant décor is as picturesque as it is sophisticated, providing a perfect atmosphere for these often decadent treats. It is, as the name suggests, flirting with you through its tables with fresh flowers and romantic serenades spilling from the speakers.

Its location in this bourgeoning district and proximity to the galleries of University Circle make it perfect for starting or winding down a pleasant evening with a sweet bite. Celebrate with a bottle of champagne bubbly or one of their craft beers. Fresh oysters and meat and cheese boards are also available for nibbles.

11607 Euclid Ave., Cleveland
216-331-2841, coquettepatisserie.com

SAVOR THE FLAVOR OF OHIO APPLES
AT GRIFFIN CIDER HOUSE

Ohio is known for its wealth of orchards, so it only makes sense to press our delicious apples into one of our favorite hard beverages. The farm-to-pint momentum, especially surrounding ciders, is full steam ahead and Richard Read of Griffin Cider has led the way in Cleveland with his English-style varieties.

The Britain native launched Griffin Cider Works to begin brewing ciders he found in his former countryside. As soon as he had captured the taste buds of sweet cider lovers, he opened Griffin Cider House, his Lakewood watering hole dedicated to the drink. Of course, you can get craft beers on tap too, but who needs it when you have all that cider from fresh local apples? It's as close to England as you'll get in this delightfully under-the-radar pub.

12401 Madison Ave., Lakewood
216-767-5444, griffinciderworks.com

PICK YOUR OWN PRODUCE
AT PATTERSON FRUIT FARM

Cleveland is rich in agriculture—just look at all our farmers's markets—so of course, every year we love to pick our own fresh fruits. Patterson Fruit Farms allows families to do just that, which is why it's become a fall tradition to climb on a wagon and ride out to the trees. Patterson also allows for strawberry picking when they are in season and all the fruits are suitable for canning and freezing to have year-round.

There are other types of family fun at the farm, too. During festivals, kids can play in hay stacks, wander around cornfield mazes, and climb into the tree house. Wagon rides remain a big attraction, because what would a trip to the farm be without horses and ponies?

8765 Mulberry Rd., Chesterland
440-729-9809, pattersonfarm.com

SAMPLE
OH-SO-CLEVELAND CUISINE

Cleveland will forever be known for the messy and marvelous union of kielbasa, French fries, coleslaw and barbecue sauce. Swing by the Seti's truck and pile chili and cheese on your sausage sandwich, or travel down the road to the legendary Hot Sauce Williams and add some of their "special sauce." Want it extra meaty? Try the Polish Girl at Williams, their spin on the perennial favorite, decked with pulled pork. For the kraut-topped variety, head to the Little Polish Diner in Parma.

Seti's Polish Boys, 3500 Woodland Ave., Cleveland
216-240-0745, setispolishboys.biz

Hot Sauce Williams, 7815 Carnegie Ave., Cleveland
216-391-2230

Little Polish Diner, 5772 Ridge Rd., Parma
440-842-8212

EAT A PACZKI
ON FAT TUESDAY

You know Lent starts the next day and you'll have to give up everything good in the world. So, that means on Fat Tuesday you may as well get as decadent as humanly possible. In Cleveland, lining up early for deep fried, jelly-filled Polish pastries called paczki is our time-honored tradition when it comes to indulging. Visit Slavic Village's bakeries, like Seven Roses, where they work overtime the week of Lent to make sure cases are lined with the gooey, powder-topped treats. Check out Parma's Eastern European bakery, Rudy's Strudel, for polka DJs.

Seven Roses, 6301 Fleet Ave., Cleveland
216-641-5789

Rudy's Strudel & Bakery, 5580 Ridge Rd., Parma
440-886-4430, rudystrudel.com

Kiedrowski's Simply Delicious Bakery, 2267 Cooper Foster Park Rd., Amherst
440-282-2700, kiedrowskibakery.com

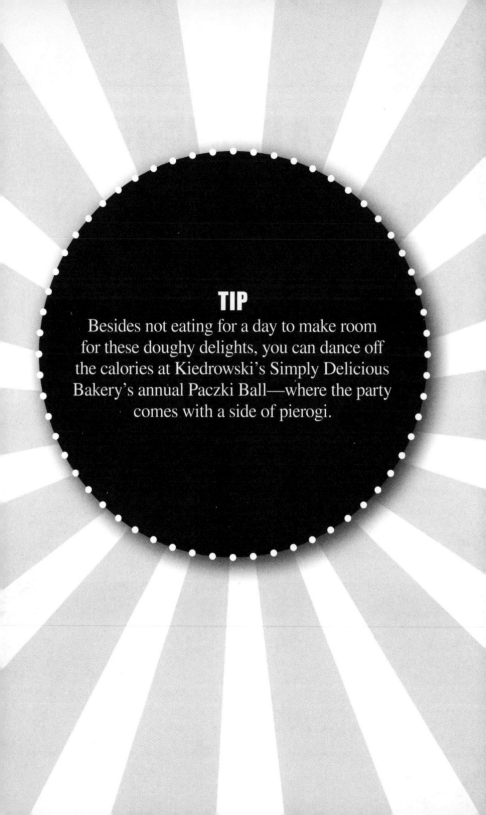

TIP

Besides not eating for a day to make room for these doughy delights, you can dance off the calories at Kiedrowski's Simply Delicious Bakery's annual Paczki Ball—where the party comes with a side of pierogi.

TAKE A BEHIND-THE-SCENES TOUR
OF GREAT LAKES BREWING COMPANY AND CAMPBELL'S SWEET FACTORY

Cleveland is churning out some of the most acclaimed food and drinks in the country and the best part is you can see exactly where all the magic happens. Start at the Beer Symposium of Great Lakes Brewing Company, the Ohio City brewery founded in 1988, where you'll meander through beer history the best possible way: with a beverage in your hand. It's the next best thing to a Christmas Ale launch party.

Trade in the smell of spelt for the aroma of candy at Campbell's Sweet Factory. Channel your inner Willy Wonka and peer into the factory where this local treasure churns out popcorn and treats. At the end, dip your own popcorn balls into decadent chocolate. On your way out, grab some Dichotomy Corn, their signature cheese-coated caramel corn.

Great Lakes Brewing Company Brewery Tour, 1951 W 26th St.
216-325-7852, greatlakesbrewing.com

Campbell's Sweet Factory Tour, 1979 W 25th St., Cleveland
216-965-0451, campbellssweets.com

TIP

After touring Great Lakes, sip brews in the basement, where you'll be among the fermenters and their small-batch, barrel-aging operation.

WATCH SAP TURN TO SYRUP
AT BURTON LOG CABIN

Ohio is known for its short but sweet maple sugaring season. But the fleeting harvest also yields some of the most delectable sap in the states. The Burton Log Cabin has carried on the tradition each spring since 1931, when the sugar house was built as a replica of Abraham Lincoln's own cabin in Kentucky. There's something comforting about the act of heating sap to a crackle in a log cabin while steam separates the water from the sap's natural sugar and expels the warm scents into the air. Burton's goes through the delicate creation of syrup every spring and churns out maple sugar year-round. Because maple sugaring requires a warmer-than-winter temperature to make the sap begin to flow, it's our yearly reminder that spring has arrived.

14590 E Park St., Burton
440-834-4204, store.burtonchamberofcommerce.org

HAVE DINNER
WITH A VIEW

The cliffside seafood gem Pier W has been serving up unparalleled views of downtown and the lake for the better part of the last century. While it's known for its upscale, sophisticated dining, it also boasts one of the best happy hours in town.

Take a seat on the patio of LockKeepers, a comfortable but classy Italian destination in Independence, where you'll look out over the historic Ohio & Erie Canal.

Laidback eatery The Harp mixes traditional Irish food and pub fare while live music adds to the spirited atmosphere. Try any of their eclectic varieties of boxty (a traditional Irish potato pancake) while you take in the view of Lake Erie.

Casual neighborhood favorite Hoopples offers a panoramic view of the downtown skyline. Regular performances by the Schwartz Brothers have become a legendary piece of local nightlife.

Pier W, 12700 Lake Ave., Lakewood
216-228-2250, pierw.com

LockKeepers, 8001 Rockside Rd., Cleveland
216-524-9404, lockkeepers.com

The Harp, 4408 Detroit Ave., Cleveland
216-939-0200, the-harp.com

Hoopples, 1930 Columbus Rd., Cleveland
216-575-0483, hoopples.com

GO THROUGH THE LUNCH LINE
AT SOKOLOWSKI'S UNIVERSITY INN

The deep roots of Eastern European immigrants in Cleveland have given rise to some of our most iconic cuisine. No time spent in Cleveland is complete without a pass through the cafeteria line of the family-owned Polish paradise Sokolowski's. This James Beard Foundation Award-winning classic has been serving up piping hot pierogi for nearly a century; it was planted in Tremont long before it was the trendy district it is today. Cleveland's love for this institution speaks volumes about our pride in time-honored tradition. Not only do we crave the diversity of Sokolowski's comfort food on one block and the inventive, chic dishes from the likes of Michael Symon and Zack Bruell a block over, we hold them all with a similar level of endearment.

1201 University Rd., Cleveland
216-771-9236, sokolowskis.com

REDISCOVER THE FLATS

The Flats are back. Family friendly during the day and adult playground at night, you can now dine, drink, or dance around the waterfront—or do all three. Come to Portside Distillery and Brewery for the tailgate Bloody Marys and stay for the award-winning infused craft rum. For something more low-key, The Willeyville farm-to-table restaurant is the Flat's foodie paradise. Or come to the Alley Cat Oyster Bar where renowned chef Zack Bruell's industrial chic eatery pairs well with the waterfront views. Part nightclub, part pool party—finish the night at FWD.

Portside Distillery and Brewery, 983 Front Ave., Cleveland
216-586-6633, portsidedistillery.com

The Willeyville, 1051 W 10th St., Cleveland
216-862-6422, thewilleyville.com

Alley Cat Oyster Bar, 1056 Old River Rd., Cleveland
216-574-9999, alleycatoysterbar.com

FWD Day and Nightclub, 1176 Front Ave., Cleveland
216-417-6282, fwdnightclub.com

DOUBLE DIP
ON LOCAL ICE CREAM AT SWEET MOSES AND MASON'S CREAMERY

Stray from the arts and bar scene of Gordon Square into Sweet Moses and you may feel like you've been teleported to another era. Soda baristas pour fizzy phosphates from behind a red counter that recalls "Happy Days" past. Mile-high sundaes are being devoured around antique parlor tables. The treats served in this old-fashioned fountain are as charming as they are delicious.

In Ohio City, Mason's Creamery is the kind of place that will remember your name and favorite ice cream every time you stop in. Just as memorable as the friendly neighborhood service are the creative, small batch, artisan flavors that change not only with the seasons, but keeps you on your toes from day to day. Where else will you find flavors like Shirley Temple sorbet or vegan Horchata?

Sweet Moses, 6800 Detroit Ave., Cleveland
216-651-2202, sweetmosestreats.com

Mason's Creamery, 4401 Bridge Ave., Ohio City
216-245-8942, masonscreamery.com

TIP

Unexpected as it may sound in an ice cream parlor, Mason's Creamery ramen nights serve up some of the best bowls of pork-bone broth and vegetarian ramen in the city. Stay tuned to their active—and charming—Facebook page for announcements.

GET A TASTE OF ITALIAN
IN LITTLE ITALY

Heat emanates from the streets of Little Italy in mid-August as swarms of food lovers descend upon the neighborhood for the Feast of the Assumption, or just "The Feast" as locals call it.

Locals head for one of Cleveland's oldest restaurants, Guarino's, which was once a Prohibition destination where liquor was served in coffee cups. It's still just as old-school, from its red sauce pasta to its lush yet kitschy décor.

Our city put its own special spin on cassata cake by swapping out ricotta and candied fruit for custard and strawberry filling and we're also known for perfecting coconut bars. You can pick up both at Corbo's Bakery.

In the summer months surrounding The Feast, have a quick brunch at the bustling Presti's, then walk across the street and watch bocce tournaments on the outdoor courts of Alta House Social Settlement.

For pasta with a side of serenading, head to La Dolce Vita for their opera nights. Singers belt out traditional and contemporary tunes with breaks in between for chit-chat.

Feast of the Assumption
holy-rosary.org/about-the-feast

Guarino's
12309 Mayfield Rd,, Cleveland, 216-231-3100
guarinoscleveland.com

Corbo's Bakery
12210 Mayfield Rd,, Cleveland, 216-421-8181
corbosbakery.net

Alta House Social Settlement
12510 Mayfield Rd,, Cleveland, 216-421-1536
altahouse.org

La Dolce Vita
12112 Mayfield Rd,, Cleveland, 216-721-8155
ladolcevitamurrayhill.com

VISIT ASIATOWN

The annual Asian Festival is just a sampling of the treasures of this district. These are a few places to get started.

Carts travel up and down the aisles of Li Wah restaurant each weekend, which allows you to pick and choose small bites like steamed buns, dumplings, and sesame balls.

In the summer, crowds gather along the lit up block after sunset as AsiaTown restaurant owners sell street food from carts. It's prime time for the discovery of the district's delicious offerings, which still fly under the radar for many locals.

The only Kwan Lion Dance troupe in Ohio has performed the vibrant traditional Chinese dance for three decades and can be found throughout the city at restaurants and events to ring in the Lunar New Year.

Li Wah, 2999 Payne Ave., Cleveland
216-589-9552, liwahrestaurant.com

Night Market Cleveland, Rockwell Ave., Cleveland
nightmarketcle.com

Kwan Lion Dance
facebook.com/Kwan-Lion-Dance-271823607012

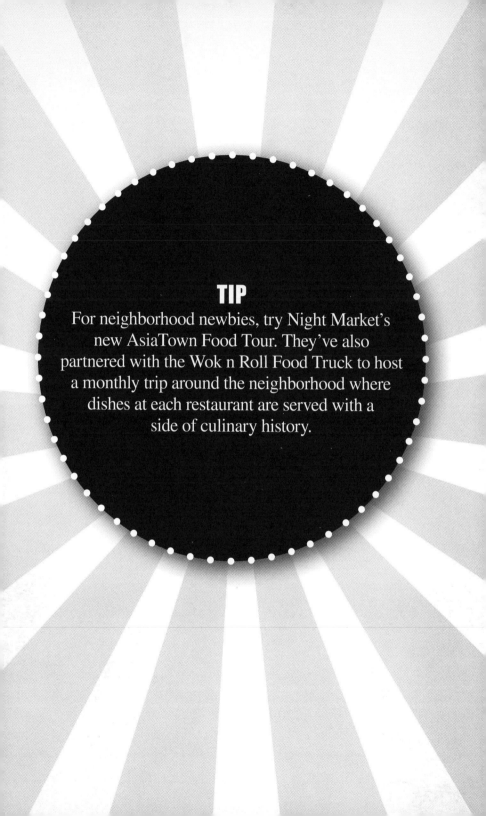

TIP

For neighborhood newbies, try Night Market's new AsiaTown Food Tour. They've also partnered with the Wok n Roll Food Truck to host a monthly trip around the neighborhood where dishes at each restaurant are served with a side of culinary history.

MUSIC AND ENTERTAINMENT

CELEBRATE
BOTH COLD AND WARM DAYS
IN WADE OVAL

The green space of culture-rich University Circle is bursting with activity in the sweltering dog days of summer and the coldest of winter. In warmer months, the sun smiles down on Wade Oval Wednesday, where live music from local musicians, dancing, and food vendors turn the park into a party.

Parade the Circle, the annual extravaganza organized by Cleveland Museum of Art, is a vibrant fusion of international and local artists. Spectacular costumes, brightly colored floats, and everything from stilt-walkers to puppets make this one of the wildest outdoor celebrations of the year.

Of course, native Clevelanders know that the cold doesn't slow us down. We just lace up our ice skates and twirl around the rink of this twinkling winter wonderland.

1 Wade Oval Dr., Cleveland, 216-791-3900
universitycircle.org

TIP

At Wade Oval Wednesday, bring a blanket for the grassy seating and an empty stomach for all the food vendors.

GET A BACKSTAGE TOUR
AT GOTTA GROOVE RECORDS AND EARTHQUAKER DEVICES

Gotta Groove is the only fully vertically integrated record manufacturing operation in the world, and its pressing plant is right here in Cleveland. Take a tour of this factory of colorful sights and sounds with the wizards of wax to see just how your favorite band's vinyl is made before you drop the needle on it.

Since 2004, Akron's EarthQuaker Devices has been crafting guitar effect pedals for some of music's biggest names. They even have a delay pedal named after the late, great Cedar Point roller coaster Disaster Transport. With bands like Modest Mouse and Speedy Ortiz among the gear's devotees, it's worth dropping in for the chance to see just where all the magic happens.

Gotta Groove Records, 3615 Superior Ave., Cleveland
800-295-0171, gottagrooverecords.com

EarthQuaker Devices, 328 Bishop St., Akron
330-252-9220, earthquakerdevices.com

TIP

Two members of the Gotta Groove staff have spun off their own experimental vinyl art project, Wax Mage. They have one of Cleveland's most popular Instagram accounts at @WaxMageRecords.

SPEND YOUR THIRD FRIDAY
AT 78TH STREET STUDIOS

Tucked away in a converted 1905 automobile factory, 78th Street Studios becomes the buzzing heartbeat of the art scene every third Friday of the month.

Make your way to favorites like Kokoon Arts Gallery and HEDGE Gallery, then check out the new spaces now inhabited by renowned illustrator Derek Hess and the offbeat peculiarities of Pugsley's Room. You can even thumb through experimental records at Bent Crayon or take in a play at Blank Canvas Theatre.

To wind down, make your way to the third floor for Popeye Gallery at Survival Kit, where festivities continue a little later into the night. The gallery, which doubles as a recording studio churning out some of the best recordings in Cleveland, hosts monthly performances where everything from experimental to classical to folk music fills the room.

1300 W 78th St., Cleveland, 330-819-7280
78thstreetstudios.com

GET BEHIND THE SCENES
AT MONSTER DRAWING RALLY

The SPACES are loaded and more than one hundred artists are up to bat. By that it means that three dozen local artists each have an hour to create a masterpiece on the spot, and then another group rotates in, and this high-energy live drawing spectacular continues through the night. And you're invited to come watch all the magic unfold.

You'll recognize the signature styles from across the city that we've come to know and love. Rarely do we get to watch the behind-the-scenes process of our favorite artists, but Monster Drawing Rally demystifies all that. Ever wonder what goes on behind studio doors? You'll see it all created in front of your eyes. And, of course, after the works are complete, they're all up for sale.

2900 Detroit Ave., Cleveland
spacesgallery.org

TAKE A STREET ART TOUR OF THE CITY
WITH CLEVELAND SGS STREET ART, ZOETIC WALLS, AND INTER|URBAN

You can learn a lot about a city from what's written on its walls. In fact, Cleveland's street art can offer one of the greatest self-guided tours taking you to new corners and telling stories through ways that only art can.

You may see the work of Cleveland SGS without realizing it, like worn and torn black and yellow signage along St. Clair-Superior that, without a closer look, could be mistaken for an auto repair shop if it wasn't advertising "Spiritual Alignment Service." Their work is as enigmatic as the identities of the collective, which are kept completely private, and add a spark of mysticism that you only notice by slowing down to take in your surroundings.

The creative hub of the Waterloo district has never been quiet about their appreciation for art. These larger-than-life murals are quirky, eclectic, and often jarring, just like the work within the neighborhood's galleries themselves.

Taking the Regional Transit Authority (RTA) is one of the best ways to see the city and the INTER|URBAN project just made it even more colorful. Hop on the Red Line to take in art installations

• •

by local and international artists. Their work takes inspiration from Cleveland's Anisfield-Wolf Book Awards, which are given to writers who explore diversity within their work.

Cleveland SGS, cobras.clevelandsgs.com

Zoetic Walls, waterlooarts.org/zoetic-walls

INTER|URBAN, riderta.com, land-studio.org

• •

CELEBRATE THE STAGE
IN TWO THEATER DISTRICTS

Make no mistake, Playhouse Square was already impressive without its twenty-foot-tall, spangling jewel against the sky, but now we can also claim a stake to the world's largest outdoor chandelier. It's one of the largest theater districts in the country, after all, but a glitzy forty-two hundred jewels don't do a thing to dim its shine. Snap a photo beneath the stunning homage to the 1920s era in which Playhouse Square was built before ducking in for a play.

If you're looking to venture outside of Playhouse Square, we have another little theater district just over the bridge in Gordon Square. Visit the cutting-edge Cleveland Public Theatre, off-the-wall Blank Canvas Theatre in 78th Street Studios, youth-driven Talespinner Children's Theatre, and culturally diverse Near West Theatre.

Playhouse Square, 1501 Euclid Ave., Suite 200, Cleveland
216-241-6000, playhousesquare.org

Cleveland Public Theatre, 6415 Detroit Ave., Cleveland
216-631-2727, cptonline.org

Blank Canvas Theatre, 1305 W 78th St., Suite 211, Cleveland
440-941-0458, blankcanvastheatre.com

Near West Theatre, 6702 Detroit Ave., Cleveland
216-961-6391, nearwesttheatre.org

Talespinner Children's Theatre, 5209 Detroit Ave., Cleveland
216-264-9680, talespinnerchildrenstheatre.org

TIP
See the most cutting-edge new works at Cleveland Public Theatre's annual Black Box series.

TAKE IN ART AND ARCHITECTURE
AT THE CLEVELAND MUSEUM OF CONTEMPORARY ART

It seems no one can pass by the sleek, glossy home of Northeast Ohio's only contemporary art museum without snapping a photo in its reflective shell. Your selfies certainly don't go unnoticed as indelible cool points, but it's what's inside that matters. The interior is equally enigmatic, a sheer feat of architecture by world-renowned designer Farshid Moussavi. The museum has hosted everything from installations of Do Ho Suh's painstaking and vibrantly hued home models to presentations of regional talent. It's also a hub of activity, just like its Uptown location, which features outdoor concerts and indoor speakers and performers like Saul Williams. Anyone who's passed through its doors and explored the multi-sensory exhibitions quickly realizes why it's a cornerstone of the Cleveland art scene.

11400 Euclid Ave., Cleveland, 216-421-8671
mocacleveland.org

TIP
On the first Saturday of every month admission to the museum is free.

PARADE THE STREETS
WITH FUZZY MONSTERS AT THE CLEVELAND KURENTOVANJE

Ten-foot-tall fuzzy white monsters known as Kurents march through the streets of the St. Clair-Superior neighborhood in Cleveland's own rendition of this popular Slovenian festival. The glittering, bright mythological giants are meant to chase away winter and welcome spring, so the masses are encouraged to bundle up and gather together to help with this task on the chilly weekend before Mardi Gras.

Cleveland has one of the largest Slovenian populations in the world and the Kurentovanje is one whimsical way to celebrate it. To stay warm post-parading, the festivities continue inside the Slovenian National Home, where music fills the century-old hall and the crowds dance alongside the Kurents. Traditional ethnic eats like strudel and krofe donuts sweeten the deal.

clevelandkurentovanje.com

MAKE PAPER
AT MORGAN CONSERVATORY

The art of papermaking may feel all but lost in the modern world, but at this east side shrine it's alive and thriving. The Morgan Conservatory is the largest arts center in the country dedicated to papermaking, book arts, and letterpress printing. On any given day, dyed papers may be hanging from the ceiling, cutting boards will be scattered along tables, and letterpresses will be turning poetry into poster art. The colorful menagerie of paper is enough to draw you into the unique space for a free visit, but don't be surprised if you fall madly in love with the medium. Hands-on workshops that are always filled to the brim prove that this art isn't going anywhere any time soon.

1754 E 47th St., Cleveland
216-361-9255, morganconservatory.org

TAKE IN AN
ART INSTALLATION
AT ROOMS TO LET

Give artists entire houses to transform into works of art and you'll understand the sheer magnitude of Rooms to Let. Attendees of this weekend event can roam through the Slavic Village neighborhood and walk inside homes that have become walk-through art installations. The results are otherworldly when you see everyday rooms completely morphed into experiential spaces. Some glow in the dark, others flash with video and sound installations, and nearly all have underlying social messages from foreclosure to what makes a house a home. It's a daring concept that challenges all who enter to think outside the box, quite literally.

Slavic Village
slavicvillage.org/roomstolet

DEVELOP PHOTOS
IN THE DARKROOM OF CLEVELAND PRINT ROOM

Look up and you'll see vintage cameras lining the space of Cleveland Print Room, the only institution in the city dedicated exclusively to photography and Cleveland's only community darkroom. Tucked away downtown in the ArtCraft Building, the Print Room is nearly hidden from plain view and just waiting to be discovered. Photographers in the know, whether beginners or experts, have long taken advantage of its unique classes and workshops, like Black and White Basics and Darkroom Manipulation. At monthly Pinhole Camera Club meetings, you can build your own camera and develop the prints right in the darkroom. But you don't have to be a photographer to visit. Artist lectures and regular exhibits, which are as eclectic in range from street photography to transcontinental portraits, showcase local and international talent.

2550 Superior Ave., Cleveland, 216-401-5981
clevelandprintroom.com

TIP

Get primped before you come because you'll want to have your photo snapped in their rare, old-school, black-and-white photo booth.

BECOME A REGULAR
AT CONCERT CLUB

Local and national talent pass through our concert halls all the time, but there are plenty of special nights that have become time-honored traditions. The mid-day gathering of sonic experimentation at Noise Lunch at Now That's Class has a new theme and curator each month. At the punk rock club, noise artists play with avant-garde sounds from distorted samples to improv jazz. The award-winning farm-to-table feast at Brunch at the Beachland Ballroom and Tavern is served where bands like The Black Keys have played their first shows—you can even get your mimosas while sitting on stage. Each time, local DJs are invited to spin for diners. The 10x3 Showcase at Brother's Lounge has a simple concept that stuck. Take ten singer-songwriters and let them each play three songs. Set in a sophisticated wine bar, you're likely to hear plenty of stories behind the songs by your favorite local musicians.

Noise Lunch at Now That's Class
11213 Detroit Ave., Cleveland, 216-221-8576, nowthatsclass.net

Brunch at the Beachland Ballroom and Tavern
15711 Waterloo Rd., Cleveland, 216-383-1124, beachlandballroom.com

10x3 Showcase at Brother's Lounge
11609 Detroit Ave., Cleveland, 216-226-2767, brotherslounge.com

TIP
While you're brunching at the Beachland,
make your way downstairs to This Way Out,
a funky, eclectic vintage shop.

SEE A PLAY
AT KARAMU HOUSE

Walk into the country's oldest African-American theater and you'll see photos spread along the wood-paneled walls. The vintage snapshots of the heyday of stars remind anyone who steps through the doors of the building's rich place in history. Established in 1915, the theater now in the Fairfax neighborhood is easily recognized by its forty-foot mural of local starlet Ruby Dee by street artist Kent Twitchell. Named for the Swahili word meaning "a place of joyful meeting," Karamu hosts an annual slate of plays as well as classes and workshops. Along with boasting successful alumni like Imani Hakim, Ron O'Neal, and Robert Guillaume, Karamu may most notably be remembered for providing a turning point in the career of rising star Langston Hughes.

2355 E 89th St., Cleveland
216-795-7070, karamuhouse.org

CATCH A FREE COMMUNITY CONCERT
BY THE CLEVELAND ORCHESTRA

Seeing the world-renowned Cleveland Orchestra at their Severance Hall home should be at the top of any Clevelander's to-do list, but we're also lucky to live in a city where the orchestra is willing to step outside of the box. Fireworks blast into the downtown skyline as the orchestra presents their annual free community concert in Public Square. The orchestra also performs weekends at its summer home Blossom Music Center from July through Labor Day weekend. During their annual neighborhood residency, musicians infiltrate communities like Lakewood, Gordon Square, and Slavic Village and perform in unconventional public places. Free concerts give Cleveland residents who may not normally seek out classical music a chance to experience the quality and versatility of the orchestra and perhaps become lifelong fans.

216-231-7300, clevelandorchestra.com

GET IN THE DIY SPIRIT
IN THE COLLINWOOD ARTS DISTRICT

The art hub is not only bursting with galleries, vintage shopping, public art, and live music, it has one of the best art walks in town, Walk All Over Waterloo. So after you've had a taste of what Waterloo Road has to offer, it's time to dive in even deeper and try something new. A satellite of the must-see Zygote Press operation, the Ink House is the only place in the region for edition printing. The home-turned-art studio opens for community printing activities, like plein air printing and neighborhood programming. Dig your hands into clay at the ceramic haven Brick Ceramics. In classes ranging from novice to intermediate—and even an expert-level open studio—you'll mold your own creations, glaze them, and fire them up in the kiln. With more than a dozen looms, Praxis Fiber Workshop is the place to learn about fiber arts. Community classes teach everything from dyeing techniques to weaving to spinning yarn.

Zygote Press Ink House, 423 E 156th St., Cleveland
zygotepress.com

Brick Ceramics, 420 E 161st St. Cleveland
216-744-4689, brickceramics.com

Praxis Fiber Workshop, 15301 Waterloo Rd., Cleveland
216-644-8661, praxisfiberworkshop.com

RING IN THE HOTTEST TIME OF THE YEAR
WITH SUMMER SOLSTICE

Ask a Northeast Ohioan and you're likely to hear that Summer Solstice—or as Clevelanders say, "Solstice"—is the party of the year. The vibrant eclectic bash heralds the sweltering beginning of summer with an all-out, steaming, wild celebration at the Cleveland Museum of Art. World music is brought in from across the globe for a heart-thumping soundtrack. The museum's outdoor plaza is transformed into a dance floor and vivid visual projects display against its soaring architecture. The dancing through the terrace, cocktail swilling in the gorgeous atrium, and traversing between the corners of galleries swell long into the night. It's not only a celebration of the changing of seasons but also a showcasing of the globe-trotting treasures within our world-class museum.

11150 East Blvd., Cleveland, 216-421-7350
clevelandart.org

HEAR EXPERIMENTAL SOUNDS
AT ALLGOSIGNS

It's hard to call the production moniker behind many of the boldest arts events around town one of the city's best kept secrets, but it is. AllGoSigns is the engineering force behind Ingenuity Fest, FireFish Festival, and Lottery League, among others. Yet AllGoSigns has consistently held many of the most under-the-radar, avant-garde performances over the last decade at its own warehouse space, including the monthly "1 Way."

Regional and national dance, visual, and musical artists have passed through this warehouse venue. From free jazz to spoken word, the intermittent shows have drawn a cult following for its evenings of experimentation. They're always weird, otherworldly, and wonderful—an excuse to break completely free of your comfort zone.

1935 W 96th St., Cleveland
allgosigns.com

PREDICT THE WEATHER
AT WOOLLYBEAR FESTIVAL

The oddball Woollybear Festival is the largest one-day festival in Ohio. Founded by former weather personality Dick Goddard, it takes its name from fuzzy caterpillar-like creatures. So you can bet people come costumed as the furry critters. Sound wacky enough yet? Every fall, thousands pack Vermillion for this family event. Not only does it include a massive parade with high school marching bands from across the state, there's even a "Woollybear 500" race where the animals go head to head. It's said that woollybears have a mystical ability to predict the winter weather ahead—and who could make us believe that's true better than the legendary Goddard? But if the black band on its back is wide and we have a full season of blizzards ahead, don't say we didn't warn you.

Vermillion, OH
vermilionchamber.net/festivals/woolybear

GET REEL
WITH LOCAL CINEMA

Everyone knows what it's like to get your hands on a Cleveland International Film Festival guide and pore over each synopsis, mark down your favorites, and plot your schedule. The festival is known for bringing in renowned and emerging worldwide talent, but it also shines with hometown pride by curating selections by local and regional directors. Cleveland Cinematheque (inside the Cleveland Institute of Art) is known for edgy, experimental, and cutting-edge films you can't see anywhere else in the region. Not only is Cedar Lee Theatre a beloved arthouse favorite to find indie flicks, it's also known for special screenings that turn up the kitsch, like monthly *Rocky Horror Picture Show* screenings. The stylish Nightlight Cinema in the heart of downtown Akron has only one tiny auditorium, but with a bar and concessions area, it's a place where fans can gather over cocktails to watch either avant-garde or more mainstream independent films.

Cleveland International Film Festival
216-623-3456, clevelandfilm.org

Cleveland Cinematheque, 11610 Euclid Ave., Cleveland
216-421-7450, cia.edu/cinematheque

Cedar Lee Theatre, 2163 Lee Rd., Cleveland Heights
216-321-5411, clevelandcinemas.com

The Nightlight, 30 N High St., Akron
330-252-5782, nightlightcinema.com

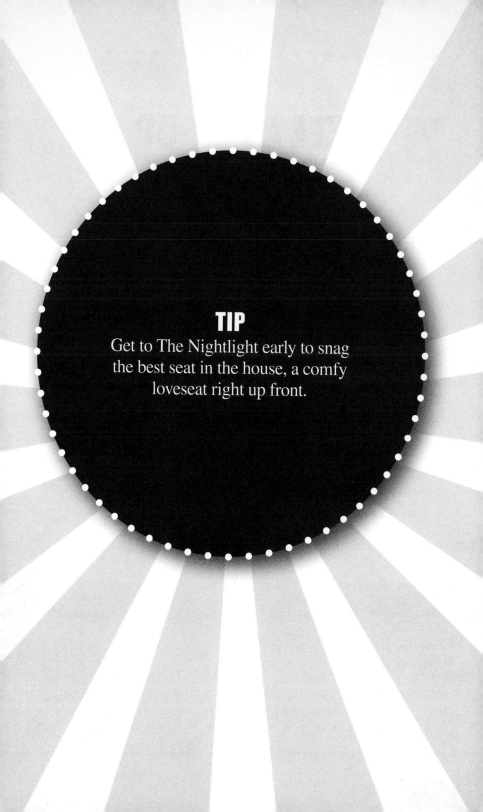

TIP
Get to The Nightlight early to snag the best seat in the house, a comfy loveseat right up front.

SEE A POP-UP PERFORMANCE
BY THEATER NINJAS

These nomadic performers are at the forefront of experimental theater. Theater Ninjas take up residency in unexpected places, such as the maze-like set-up of *Black Cat Lost* in 78th Street Studios or the artistic, bohemian Negative Space Gallery for *The Grand Celebration of the Celestial Mystery*. But they don't just pop up in unique spaces, they completely transform them. Meanwhile, the line between audience and actor disappears. *Codes*, inspired by the life of Alan Turing, took guests through a series of different interactive installations, such as one where selfies of the actors and participants were tweeted to the public. Rife with thoughtful social commentary, shows are often a *Choose Your Own Adventure*-style theatrical experience that places you right in the middle of the action.

theaterninjas.com

GET LUCKY
AT THE ST. PATRICK'S DAY PARADE

Fill up with a great big Irish breakfast, because this parade doesn't hold back any punches—Cleveland was the home of Irish boxing champ Kilbane, after all. Cleveland has the largest St. Patrick's Day parade in the nation outside of Boston.

Set your clocks to 1:04 p.m., the exact time the parade steps off each year. Whether you march through the streets with the floats and dancers or watch from the sidelines as the sea of green passes you by, it's one of the most unique ways to see downtown.

And should you happen to need a pint of Guinness, look no farther than Flat Iron Cafe, the city's oldest Irish pub. Try Moriarty's for a dive off the beaten path and Flannery's Pub for a more high-octane affair.

stpatricksdaycleveland.com

TIP
Be on the lookout for the bagpipe band Cleveland Firefighters Memorial Pipes and Drums making appearances in bars and restaurants throughout the city.

ATTEND
A MUSIC FESTIVAL

The Cleveland music scene has been named one of the top in the country, so it makes sense to have such great festivals shining a spotlight on our talent.

Brite Winter was created as a way to show that we're not afraid of a little cold and snow. Bundle up, put on some mittens, and see bands take over indoor and outdoor venues throughout the sprawling festival. If you get a little chilly, just pop a marshmallow on a stick and huddle around the open pit fires.

Ingenuity Fest has always been about experimentation and pushing the envelope. Every year, the art and technology festival pops up in underutilized and unexpected spaces for a weekend of entertainment and innovation.

College radio is alive and well at Case Western Reserve University. Studio-A-Rama has always been the show of the summer. Every year, local bands and plenty of noteworthy headliners rock out on stage.

Brite Winter, britewinter.com

Ingenuity Fest, ingenuitycleveland.com

Studio-A-Rama, wruw.org

DANCE THE NIGHT AWAY

It don't mean a thing if it ain't got that swing. Put on your dancing shoes and travel back to a time when the Charleston and Balboa ruled the floor. You'll feel like you've time-travelled to another era at Get Hep Swing's twice-a-month public swing dances, where jitterbugs of all skill levels are welcome to jump and jive.

At Touch Supper Club, the speakeasy-like basement is a landmark of Cleveland nightlife. Descend the stairs of the posh urban eatery to a dance floor presided over by local DJs. Eclectic is the name of the game here. Themed nights throughout the week—from soul to indie to old-school hip-hop—pack crowds looking for diverse tracks spun by true music aficionados.

Get Hep Swing
gethepswing.com

Touch Supper Club, 2710 Lorain Ave., Cleveland
216-631-5200, touchsupperclub.com

SPOT RISING ARTISTIC TALENT
AT THE CLEVELAND INSTITUTE OF ART'S DESIGN SHOW

While its big, beautiful new addition in Uptown reminds passersby that the college is pumping out the best and brightest artists, many Clevelanders aren't as familiar with the innovation within, particularly when it comes to the design department. CIA is largely regarded as one of the top three schools in the country for automotive and graphic design and interior architecture.

That's why big-name businesses scout out new talent at CIA's annual design show, which is open to the public. Students present their fresh perspectives on the new wave of product design and visual artistry. Looking for what's next in flashy, cutting-edge sports cars? The most intriguing restaurant design concepts? Let your imagination run wild at this showcase of the future.

11610 Euclid Ave., Cleveland
800-223-4700, cia.edu

EXPERIENCE THE CIRCUS
UNDER A TINY TENT WITH WIZBANG!

There's no telling where this tiny roving tent of variety circus mayhem will pop up next. Imagine all the off-kilter sideshow acts possible rolled into one quirky extravaganza under a fully-functional big top with an 8′ x 8′ stage and you have WizBang! With a healthy dose of neo-vaudevillian entertainment and cabaret, expect a full-on sensory overload with the assistance of accordions, slapstick humor, and juggling acts. Pull back the velvet curtains and prepare to be dazzled with Hula-Hoops, mimes, and magic tricks. Between the zany costumes and all-out eccentricities, don't be surprised if they call on you for a little audience participation. With only about sixty seats per show, it may just be your lucky day.

wizbangtheatre.com

CHANNEL YOUR INNER HIPPIE
AT HESSLER STREET FAIR

Align your chakras, pull on your best tie-dye shirt or hemp dress, and put on your patchouli oil. Shimmy down to Hessler Road on the one weekend a year it turns into the biggest block party in the city. Poetry is recited, street performers belly dance and juggle through the swarm of people, and roots and reggae bands play to the crowds at this brick road hippie fest. You'll find barefoot jewelry makers and long-haired antique sellers peddling groovy handmade arts and crafts in the true old-school sense of the words. If the party vibe gets to be too much, just steal away to Barking Spider Tavern and sit on the patio under the stars.

Hessler Road, hesslerstreetfair.org

LEARN SOMETHING NEW
AT THE ROCK & ROLL HALL OF FAME'S
EDUCATION PROGRAMS

Since Cleveland disc jockey Alan Freed uttered the words "rock and roll," music has been in our fair city's bloodline. It's no stretch to say the Rock Hall, brimming with floor after floor of pop culture artifacts, is our landmark. Whether tracking down the handwritten lyrics to Neil Young's "Heart of Gold" or admiring the over-the-top outfits of Michael Jackson, you can spend an entire day perusing the collections.

But for a lesser-known reason you should be sticking around the Hall after hours. Attend their free programs, where their expert staff tackle everything from rock history to modern-day pop music, often through live interviews with Hall of Fame Inductees. Spend the evening tracing the roots of prog rock or rediscovering the protest songs of the Vietnam War. It'll hold you over between attending the HOF inductions held here every two years.

1100 E 9th St., Cleveland
216-781-7625, rockhall.com

SEE DOUBLE
AT THE TWINS DAYS FESTIVAL

Your eyes don't deceive you. Those are really thousands of sets of twins descending upon Twinsburg's fairgrounds. And with a name like that, there's no better place to host the world's largest assembly of twins. But don't worry, non-twins are just as welcome to the spectacle.

For forty years, siblings have descended on the town to mix and mingle. The gathering has a twins parade, talent show, and competition—think, awards for most alike and least alike. And, of course, the unspoken rule is that everyone paired up must be dressed alike. That makes for double the fun when it comes to zany costumes and cosplay. With people coming in from all over the globe, Twinsburg truly becomes the epicenter of twins—even if just for one day.

Downtown Twinsburg
330-425-3652, twinsdays.org

BRING OUT YOUR BELLY LAUGH
AT ACCIDENTAL COMEDY CLUB

Cleveland's indie comedy scene has grown in spades over the last decade, and that's largely due to the valiant efforts of Accidental Comedy Club. Beyond their showcases of locals, the curators are known for bringing in up-and-coming out-of-towners on the cusp of exploding.

Their programming has given stand-up a presence around town by constantly bringing new shows to new places, like Great Lakes Brewing Company's basement and Happy Dog. Their pop-up "secret" shows have brought big names to some of the coolest hidden gems in Cleveland, like the stellar, must-see Nash on 80th in Slavic Village. Ever wanted to see a comedian perform on the rooftop of the Cleveland Hostel with the city skyline as their backdrop? It's a good look—for the audience and the community.

accidentalcomedy.com

CELEBRATE FREE COMIC BOOK DAY
AT CAROL & JOHN'S COMIC BOOK SHOP

There's a reason local artists consider co-owner John Dudas a real Cleveland superhero. Sure, Cleveland loves its comics and its comic stores, but we'd be remiss to say Carol & John's isn't so much more.

You can catch comic book lovers and collectors lining up at midnight for the national celebration of Free Comic Book Day. But inside, you'll also see local illustrators at tables passing out their own creations. With so many artists in one place, creativity is bound to transpire. That's why it's been the jump-off point for many of our favorite artistic collaborations to date. And if you need any more reason to stop in, their lovable orange cat Winston is a creature of legend.

17462 Lorain Ave., Cleveland
216-252-0606, cnjcomics.com

TIP

Coming in character is more than welcome at Free Comic Book Day. In fact, cosplay is encouraged. The midnight crowd is geared more toward grown-ups, while daylight is teeming with kids.

PARTY AROUND TOWN
WITH POLKA

Cleveland loves polka so much that we're known for our own style of the dance floor filler. And don't think there's any shortage of ways to pay homage to the Old World classic. The accordions of polka legends like Frank Yakovic are on display at the Polka Hall of Fame. Learn all about the Cleveland sound that emerged from the neighborhoods filled with Polish immigrants. The zany Dyngus Day west side fest is full of polka and pierogi. March with the parade then spill into the many bars and restaurants joining in on the once-a-year extravaganza. Try Happy Dog, where polka is no stranger. Their year-round Polka Happy Hour is always wall-to-wall with fans. Sterle's Country House, a St. Clair-Superior restaurant, isn't just a destination for Slovenian comfort food. You'll regularly find live polka bands playing to diners.

Cleveland-Style Polka Hall of Fame, 605 E 222nd St., Euclid
216-261-3263, clevelandstyle.com

Dyngus Day, clevelanddyngus.com

Sterle's Country House, 1401 E 55th St., Cleveland
216-881-4181, sterlescountryhouse.com

Skinny's Bar and Grille, 780 E 222nd St., Cleveland
216-731-3443

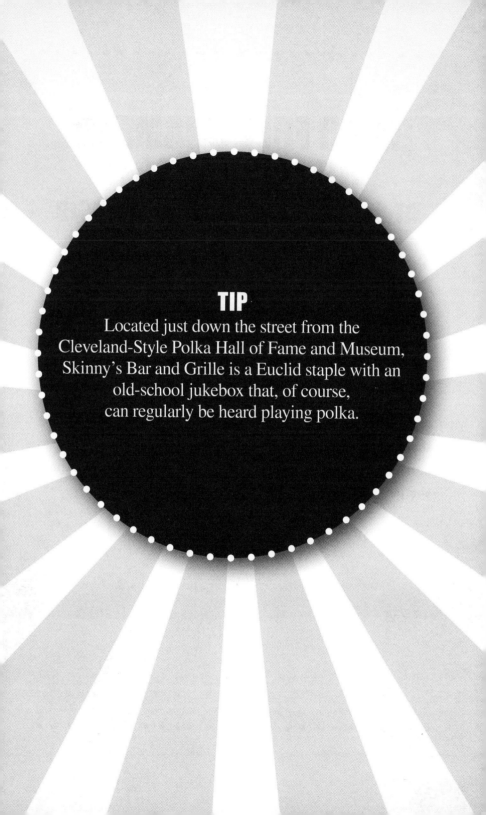

TIP

Located just down the street from the
Cleveland-Style Polka Hall of Fame and Museum,
Skinny's Bar and Grille is a Euclid staple with an
old-school jukebox that, of course,
can regularly be heard playing polka.

HEAR FREE CHAMBER MUSIC CONCERTS
AT CLEVELAND INSTITUTE OF MUSIC

Dropping in on a concert at Cleveland Institute of Music feels a bit like someone whispering a secret in your ear. Almost all concerts at this renowned conservatory are free, which makes it an undercover steal, especially for orchestral music fans. We love our Cleveland Orchestra, but we also appreciate our up-and-comers. On any given day, you'll hear the recitals of emerging talent and esteemed faculty, or ensemble performances at any of their regular series. To you it's a day out on the town; to the students, it's just practice. Take advantage of the opportunity to hear these virtuosos while it doesn't cost a penny. Before long, you may just see them gracing Severance Hall.

11021 East Blvd., Cleveland
216-791-5000, cim.edu

END YOUR NIGHT SINGING KARAOKE
AT TINA'S NITE CLUB

As the night winds down and the urge to sing your lungs out tugs harder and harder, there's only one place to go. A no-frills-to-the-core, hidden Ohio City dive, Tina's is truly off the beaten path. And that's part of what makes it so fun. You're never quite sure what you might see as the evening grows later. Pretensions are dropped and microphones picked up immediately by anyone who walks through these doors. It's not all "Sweet Caroline" here, but don't be surprised if you get pulled into a sing-along. That's just what happens when drinks are as cheap as they are here. You can be sure you'll see every walk of life at Tina's on any given night. The one constant: no matter what day it is, the karaoke machine is on.

5400 Herman Ave., Cleveland
216-651-8057

LISTEN IN
AT THE LOTTERY LEAGUE CONCERT

What happens when you put the names of dozens of local musicians into a lottery wheel, choose them at random to create completely new bands, then tell them they have two months to put together a concert? The part rock 'n roll circus, part game show, part city-wide art project that is known as Lottery League.

There's one major rule: no two musicians are allowed to have ever played together before. As you'd expect, this mishmash of match-ups challenges participants to think outside their usual genres. Classically trained harpists start collaborating with punks, rappers start playing with noise musicians. The grand finale is something called The Big Show, where all the new bands play a set in one all-day music blowout.

lotteryleague.org

TIP

Draft night, when all the bands are picked, is completely open to the public, and the epic event lets you see new bands chosen one by one.

Photo Credit: Gary Burkholder

SPORTS AND RECREATION

MONKEY AROUND
AT THE CLEVELAND METROPARKS ZOO

Want to frolic with a fennec fox or kick it with a koala? Welcome to Cleveland's hub of animal activity. And we just happen to have the largest collection of primates in North America. Watch these playful aerialists swing from tree to tree on Monkey Island, a beloved primate habitat at the zoo for more than sixty years.

A stroll through our urban safari may be a classic sunny day activity, but for the more chilly temperatures, venture into the tropical world of The Rainforest. Take a waltz through the misty jungle, where you'll see electric-hued frogs leap from rock to rock while crocodiles smile at you from the stream. And those dark, darting movements out of the corner of your eye? Those are just bats taking flights.

3900 Wildlife Way, Cleveland
216-661-6500, clevelandmetroparks.com/Zoo

WATCH THE SUNSET
FROM THE LAKEWOOD SOLSTICE STEPS

We're all a little bit guilty of taking a glorious Instagram off the edge of Lakewood Park, where the view of downtown meets the shimmering water's edge. The boardwalk is a stunning lakeside stroll where you will see runners, baby strollers, dog walkers, and skaters all spending their day in the sun.

The addition of the Lakewood Solstice Steps, a cascading cement staircase that wraps around the waterfront, makes this gathering spot even more of a new summer tradition. Along the 480 feet of coastline, you'll see couples enjoying ice cream and kids playfully trying their hardest to lift their little legs from one tall step to another. In the densely packed melting pot of Lakewood, the Solstice Steps give one more reason to bring people together.

14532 Lake Ave., Lakewood

KNOCK DOWN PINS
AT MAHALL'S

Lacing up a pair of bowling shoes and tossing a few balls down the lane is a classic family bonding experience for a Saturday night, but there's nothing average about this nearly century-old alley. This is the kind of place where you can find glittery throwback threads at Cattitude Vintage store, the perfect place to find your attire for the 90s-themed DJ night you'll be attending later.

Though Mahall's is the oldest alley in Ohio, recent renovations to their performance and event space have attracted nationally touring talent for nightly concerts. Step up to the separate bar and you can get your Mason jar filled with beer or cocktails and snack on some of the best fried chicken in town.

13200 Madison Ave., Lakewood
216-521-3280, mahalls20lanes.com

TIP
Mahall's hosts an industry brunch on Monday for anyone who wants to keep the weekend going one more day.

ESCAPE TO THE FOLIAGE
OF ROCKEFELLER PARK GREENHOUSE

Both a hidden gem and a blossoming, colorful respite to brighten even the grayest day, the Rockefeller Park Greenhouse is always bursting with flora. Located right by the Cleveland Cultural Gardens, there's a magic in finding the sprawling green space in an otherwise urban neighborhood. For over a century, Rockefeller Park has bloomed with exotic and native plants. Indoors, visitors can wander among artfully displayed plants from the tropics, Japan, and Latin America, interspersed with native seasonal varieties. Visit the outdoor gazebo of the Peace Garden in warmer temperatures. At this free hideaway that offers a quick escape from city life, you're likely to catch art students sketching, poets scribbling in notebooks, and families strolling on their day off—all in one place.

750 E 88th St., Cleveland
216-664-3103, rockefellergreenhouse.org

EXPLORE THE JEWELS
OF THE EMERALD NECKLACE

The Cleveland Metroparks, known to locals as the Emerald Necklace, represents one of the nation's largest concentrations of park land per capita.

The Chalet toboggan chutes in Cleveland Metroparks Mill Stream Run Reservation are the only public ice chutes in Ohio. Zipping down the sleek, cold structures while the cold wind whips in your face has become a winter tradition.

Hidden within Slavic Village is the tallest cascade falls in Cuyahoga County. The forty-eight-foot Mill Creek Falls is part of one of the largest tributaries to the Cuyahoga River and once powered the first grist and saw mill in the area in 1799.

Within the Rocky River Reservation, the Stinchcomb-Groth Memorial Scenic Overlook hosts free concerts for a family party in the park.

Toboggan Chutes, 16200 Valley Pkwy., Strongsville, 440-572-9990
clevelandmetroparks.com/Main/toboggan-chutes.aspx

Mill Creek Falls, 8404 Webb Terrace, Cleveland
clevelandmetroparks.com/Main/Mill-Creek-Falls.aspx

Stinchcomb-Groth Memorial Scenic Overlook
clevelandmetroparks.com/Main/Stinchcomb-Groth-Memorial-Scenic-Overlook.aspx

TRAVEL
THE TOWPATH TRAIL

Cyclists, joggers, and walkers have met their match at the Towpath Trail. Following the historic route of the Ohio & Erie Canal, there are eighty-five sprawling miles here and and every one of them has something to offer. The Flats is always one of the best places to begin exploring the city, and you'll find the newest section of the trail with industrial backdrops and a view of the skyline along Scranton Road. Breeze past wetlands and shady forests as you pass through the counties of Cuyahoga, Stark, Summit, and Tuscarawas. Those looking to break out their bikes can even ride one way and return by using the Cuyahoga Valley Scenic Railroad's Bike Aboard program. It's not only a walk through history, but a way to take in current-day Cleveland in all its lush glory.

ohioanderiecanalway.com

HIGH-SPEED CYCLE
AROUND THE CLEVELAND VELODROME

Cleveland is a bicycle city. We're bike fanatics in every sense of the word. You can find us leisurely peddling through the streets year-round, we are on a first-name basis with the owners of our beloved bicycle shops, and we show up in droves for Cleveland Critical Mass and NEO Cycle Fest.

But sometimes, we like to kick things up a notch. At the outdoor Slavic Village track, Ohio's only velodrome complex, cyclists whizz by on the 166-meter circular track and gracefully hug its fifty-degree corners. Open riding sessions are held throughout the year, and anyone looking to brush up on their riding skills can hop into an all-ages class. For a true spectator sport that warps your perception of gravity, swing by during any of their high-octane weekly races.

5033 Broadway Ave., Cleveland
216-256-4285, clevelandvelodrome.org

SOAR ABOVE THE TREETOPS
AT HOLDEN ARBORETUM

Kirtland is home to one of the world's largest arboreta. Take guided or self-guided tours through the woodlands and explore gardens, ravines, and streams. For the more daring, two more new additions cater to thrill seekers. The Kalberer Emergent Tower might just be the ultimate tree fort. Climb up 120 feet in the sky to look out over the trees for a clear view of Lake Erie. Then, assuming you're not afraid of any heights, take a stroll across the Murch Canopy Walk, a five-hundred-foot-long elevated walkway built sixty-five feet above the forest floor. You'll be right between the trees and able to have a bird's-eye view of the creatures that call Holden Arboretum their home.

9550 Sperry Rd., Kirtland
440-946-4400, holdenarb.org

RIDE THE WAVES
OF CLEVELAND'S LAKES AND RIVERS

If you're in Cleveland in the warmer months, chances are you're hanging out by the water.

Stand up paddle around Lake Erie with SUPCLE. Taking off from Edgewater Park, you can do everything from group SUP lessons to sunset paddles. For those with balance, you can even try SUP yoga.

When a leisurely canoe trip is in order, join Hiram's Camp Hi on one of their trips along twenty-five miles of the Upper Cuyahoga River.

Few things bring on the same rush as kayaking. 41 North is one of the top kayaking schools on the Great Lakes. Take a sunset tour of the Burning River, marvel at Lakewood's cliffs and coves, and explore a 1911 shipwreck during a day trip at Kelley's Island.

Stand Up Paddling, Edgewater Park
440-212-5041, supcle.com

41 North
866-529-2541, kayak41north.com

Camp Hi
330-569-7621, camphicanoe.com

GO CAMPING
AT NELSON'S LEDGES QUARRY PARK

It's a summer tradition to pack up the camper and hit the road to Nelson's Ledges. The outdoor park isn't far from Cleveland, but you'll feel like you are in another part of the world. More than four hundred campsites are scattered through the 250 acres of forested land to hike in, cliffs to view vistas from, and streams to play in or walk along. For the more adventurous, try scuba diving in the depths among the catfish and blue gills. For the rest of us, just pack the marshmallows for late night campfires. Whether just getting the gang together for the weekend or attending one of the many festivals, Nelson's has become a beloved getaway with literally "something for everyone."

12001 Nelson Ledge Rd., Garrettsville
440-548-2716, nlqp.com

TIP
If you're going to a music fest weekend and want to snag the best campsite, arrive at the site on the Thursday before the festival.

TAKE A SNOW DAY
AT CHAPIN FOREST RESERVATION

We know we have some rough winters. But being the Clevelanders that we are, you had better believe we make the best of it. In fact, we bundle up, break out our sleds and snowshoes, and head straight to Chapin Forest Reservation. Cross-country skiers can zoom through groomed trails day or night, passing by grand old trees, scenic rock formations, and ledges formed before the glaciers moved across Ohio. For something a little calmer, just rent snowshoes and follow the marked trails. And if you want to warm up between treks, just stop in to the Pine Lodge Ski Center and cozy up to the wood stove or fire pit. Then get back out on the trails. Hot cocoa can wait.

12840 Girdled Rd., Concord Twp.
lakemetroparks.com

EXPERIENCE THE ARTS
OUTDOORS THROUGH CONSERVANCY OF CUYAHOGA VALLEY NATIONAL PARK

Most Clevelanders are aware of how rich a resource for hiking and all things outdoors we have with the Cuyahoga Valley National Park being right in our own backyard. Lesser known is the Conservancy, which injects a bit of the metropolitan, big city feel into the natural world with its programming. Music fills the park with house concerts at the Hines Hill Conference Center; roots, rock, and folk musicians take over the cozy Happy Days Lodge, and live bands play open-air sets in Howe Meadow. View the rotating exhibitions of local artists on showcase at the Seiberling Gallery at the headquarters, or create art of your own by tagging along with the Cuyahoga Valley Photographic Society. With a backdrop as grand as CVNP, it's impossible not to stay inspired.

1403 W Hines Hill Rd., Peninsula
330-657-2909, conservancyforcvnp.org

FLEX
YOUR PINBALL SKILLS

The clinks and clanks of pinballs batting through brightly lit machines is music to the ears of Clevelanders. At B Side, this Coventry bar with wall-to-wall game machines is located directly under the legendary concert club Grog Shop. But that doesn't mean it lacks a life of its own. The city's best DJs spin for the dance floor and spoken-word artists have had a residency for years. Located directly across from the west side Happy Dog (which has games of its own), Superelectric might be the most colorful place in town. You'll find brightly painted walls and retro kitsch paintings like a velvet Elvis and Betty Boop. Handcrafted sodas are slurpable for little ones and big kids alike. At 16-Bit Bar and Arcade, old-school video games are everywhere. But equally as indulgent as the free play is the cocktail menu, where you'll find concoctions like the Darryl Hannah garnished with Swedish Fish or the Punky Brewster built with orange sherbet vodka.

B Side, 2785 Euclid Heights Blvd., Cleveland
216-932-1966, bsideliquorlounge.com

Superelectric Pinball Parlor, 6500 Detroit Ave., Cleveland
419-215-8797, superelectric.tv

16-Bit Bar and Arcade, 15012 Detroit Ave., Lakewood
216-563-1115, 16-bitbar.com

ROOT FOR THE HOME TEAM
WITH CLEVELAND SOFTBALL

Sure, the Cleveland Indians opening day at Progressive Field is a city-wide, firework-filled tradition, and our minor league teams are an underrated treasure. But we all know the true stars that are up to bat wear Cleveland Softball t-shirts. Volunteer-run, league fee-free, and DIY to the core, most of the teams are comprised of employees from your favorite local music venues, record stores, coffee shops, and college radio stations—in other words, true local sports heroes. If that doesn't give you a good enough idea of the antics going down every summer, just come to one of the free games at Gordon Park and see the self-proclaimed greatest co-ed softball team in the world for yourself.

SOAK UP THE FUN
AT CLEVELAND BEACHES

Whether watching the Fourth of July fireworks or having a Memorial Day picnic, Cleveland's beaches are some of our favorite hangouts. We love our waterfront—and it gives us as good an excuse as any to play in the sun.

Stop at Mentor's Headland Beach State Park's mile-long beach, which is the largest natural sand beach in Ohio. Two trails weave through the park and a breakwall allows for fishing.

You may need a local to show you how to get down to Whiskey Island, but that's part of what makes it so great. That, and the fact that the secluded park is all about beach volleyball, grilling out in the summer, and sailing.

Huntington Reservation is one of the oldest reservations in Cleveland. On its 103 acres in Bay Village is a half-mile beach and the Lake Erie Nature and Science Center.

Mentor Headlands, 9601 Headlands Rd., Mentor
440-466-8400, parks.ohiodnr.gov/headlandsbeach

Whiskey Island, 2800 Whiskey Island, Cleveland
216-631-1800, whiskeyislandmarina.net

Huntington Reservation, Wolf Picnic Area Dr., Bay Village
216-635-3200

TOUCH DOWN
AT THE PRO FOOTBALL HALL OF FAME

Football enthusiasts are more than just fans, they're known fanatics. This mecca of football history is located where the NFL was founded (then called the American Professional Football Association, for purists), which just happens to be in Canton. Walk the halls of those earliest days of the sport all the way to the current scores and stars while celebrating the careers of the retired greats and perusing the iconic memorabilia of days past. Although today we're tapped into every move of our favorite players, this shrine preserves many of the earliest artifacts we couldn't see anywhere else. Relive the days of glory through media guides that date back to the 1930s, more than one hundred scrapbooks, and a whopping three million photographic images. An absolute must for anyone with a love of the game.

2121 George Halas Dr. NW, Canton
330-456-8207, profootballhof.com

DO A LAP
AT LEAGUE PARK

Tucked away in the Hough neighborhood is the country's oldest ballpark, League Park, which dates back to 1891. Today, the Baseball Heritage Museum, once housed in the 5th Street Arcades, has been moved into the park's restored ticket booth. If browsing the artifacts doesn't take you back in history, just stand at the home plate where Babe Ruth hit his 500th home run in 1929.

But the museum itself is more than a collection of relics of America's favorite pastime. It's dedicated to celebrating the diversity of the game and the participants from all walks of life who defined it. You'll find plenty of uniforms, but you'll also find mementos of the women's league and the Cuban baseball past. Photographs, letters, and programs help tell the stories of the many players who shaped the sport.

6601 Lexington Ave., Cleveland
216-789-1083, baseballheritagemuseum.org

Photo Credit: Roger Mastroianni

CULTURE AND HISTORY

SPEAK YOUR MIND
AT THE CITY CLUB

The country's oldest, non-partisan, and continuously operating free speech forum is right in the heart of downtown Cleveland. Over a century of community gatherings, it's hosted speakers from Rosa Parks to Franklin D. Roosevelt. Today, panels and guests from around the world come to discuss the city's—and the world's—most pressing issues. The second half of each session is dedicated to taking unscripted questions from the audience to allow ideas to grow from challenging conversations. In addition to bringing in renowned authors and activists to the headquarters itself, City Club has partnered with local establishments like the Happy Dog to bring its mission to the greater public and ensure everyone has a voice in current events.

850 Euclid Ave., Suite 200, Cleveland
216-621-0082, cityclub.org

SEE WHAT'S UNDER THE SEA
AT THE CLEVELAND AQUARIUM

This may be the one time a shark floating above your head is no cause for alarm. Actually, at the Cleveland Aquarium, swimming with the finned creatures is even encouraged. But for those who prefer to stay dry, a stroll through the stunning, underwater SeaTube is a chance to get up close and personal with sharks and various other sea creatures.

In 2012, the old 1892-built FirstEnergy Powerhouse in the west bank of the Flats was transformed into Ohio's only free-standing aquarium. Half a million gallons of water later, it's home to exotic sea creatures from South America to the Red Sea to Fiji, and to plenty of life native to Ohio's own rivers and lakes as well. Watch daily fish feedings and touch stingrays.

2000 Sycamore St., Cleveland
216-862-8803, greaterclevelandaquarium.com

GET INTERGALACTIC
AT THE NASA GLENN VISITOR CENTER
AT GREAT LAKES SCIENCE CENTER

Only a few select cities across the country have NASA outposts, and Northeast Ohio is lucky enough to be the home of Glenn Research Center and Sandusky's Plum Brook Station. So for budding young astronauts, the Visitor Center is one of the closest year-round things they can do to going behind the scenes with the real deal. Scope out a real moon rock from Apollo 15, the actual 1973 Skylab 3 Apollo Command Module, and spacesuits from Skylab and Apollo.

During select months, NASA Glenn also opens its doors to the public with special guided tours where guests can see where scientists and engineers develop propulsion, power, and communication technologies. See a fully immersive, virtual reality room at Glenn's Graphics & Visualization or parts of Plum Brook Station testing stations.

601 Erieside Ave., Cleveland
216-694-2000, greatscience.com

TIP

Ask tour guides at Plum Brook Station for all the details on where parts of the *Avengers* were shot.

TAKE A LITERARY TOUR
OF CLEVELAND

Langston Hughes House: Famed playwright Langston Hughes wrote many of his earliest works in the third floor attic of this east side house. Though he eventually moved to New York City, he would regularly return to his hometown to debut his work at Karamu House.

Hart Crane Memorial Park: This waterfront park by the west bank of the Flats pays homage to the short life of Garrettsville-born poet Hart Crane. Right below the Rapid line, sculptures by Gene Kangas pay tribute to the fallen writer. In the distance, kids play on the Crooked River Skate Park under the bridge, one of the most uniquely Cleveland backdrops in the city.

Harvey Pekar Statue: Comic illustrator Harvey Pekar, author of *American Splendor* and other graphic novels, was Cleveland's own anti-hero. The bronze statue is—naturally—Pekar shrugging with the word bubble reading, "Oy vey! What do you want from my life?"

Brews and Prose: Poetry should feel as at home in a bar as it does in a library or classroom. This monthly event brings in local and national authors to read in the packed basement of Market Garden Brewery.

Loganberry Books: More than ten thousand books line the walls of this Larchmere treasure. Browse "The Sanctuary" filled with first-edition rarities and visit the Lit Arts room, where events like the annual Edible Books Festival take place.

Langston Hughes House
2266 E 86th St., Cleveland

Hart Crane Memorial Park
Columbus Rd. and Merwin Ave., Cleveland

Harvey Pekar Statue
Cleveland Heights-University Heights Library
13866 Cedar Rd., Cleveland, 216-321-4700
heightslibrary.org

Brews and Prose
1947 W 25th St., Cleveland
brewsandprose.com

Loganberry Books
13015 Larchmere Blvd., Cleveland, 216-795-9800
loganberrybooks.com

DISSECT THE HISTORY OF HEALTH
AT THE DITTRICK MUSEUM OF MEDICAL HISTORY

You don't have to be a medical aficionado to appreciate the vintage apparatuses that line the walls of the steampunk-to-the-core Dittrick. A hidden gem within the bustling Case Western Reserve University campus, this museum traces the origins of early pharmaceutical history up through today's modern marvels. That includes inventions by the university's own staff, such as the heart defibrillator and a compression chamber that was developed to assist 1900s Cleveland laborers in bringing fresh water into the city.

For yet another undiscovered treasure, enter the second floor library and find your way into the Millikin Room of Microscopes, a snug, scholarly, wood-paneled room lined from floor to ceiling with the classic instruments from bygone eras.

11000 Euclid Ave., Cleveland,
216-368-3648, artsci.case.edu/Dittrick

TAKE A WALK
AROUND THE WORLD AT THE
CLEVELAND CULTURAL GARDENS

Many zip past the sprawling greenery along Martin Luther King Boulevard on their daily commute, but few slow down to fully appreciate the twenty-six gardens, each representing different countries, that make up 254 acres. Celebrating the wealth of diversity in Cleveland, the Cultural Gardens date back to 1916 when the Shakespeare Garden was built.

The gardens that followed were equally poetic. Each elegantly decorated with features such as water fountains, sculptures, and statues from Chopin to Madame Curie, they're both an outdoor walk through history and a quiet urban oasis winding through one of Cleveland's busiest areas. Look for the dragons guarding the entrance of the Chinese Garden with a statue of Confucius. Find a bust of Beethoven in the German Garden.

750 E 88th St., Cleveland
440-446-1466, clevelandculturalgardens.org

SOAR
TO THE CREATION OF SUPERMAN

The Man of Steel is a global sensation, but he was dreamt up by two high school kids right here in the heart of Glenville. Superheroes don't always come from lands like Krypton. Sometimes, they're in our own backyards.

For fans of the city's own larger-than-life comic book star, the restored home of Jerry Siegel, who penned the original Superman stories, is a must-see. You'll know you're in the right place when you see the iconic Superman emblem outside.

A few blocks away, illustrator Joe Shuster's childhood home is appropriately commemorated with a tribute fence. Right at the corner of Lois Lane (Parkwood Drive) and Joe Shuster Lane (Amor Avenue), oversized reprints of the first Superman comic line both sides. It's also a must-see.

Superman house, 10622 Kimberley Ave., Cleveland

Superman fence, Amor Ave., Cleveland

SHOUT
FROM THE ROOFTOPS

Sometimes it's nice to see the city from a different point of view. The first place to make your way to is Tower City. Soaring forty-two floors in the sky, the mall's observation deck oversees not only the city, but the new renovations to Public Square. Stay tuned to the colorful official Twitter account #TowerCityCLE, which keeps you up-to-date on events, like special lighting that makes for breathtaking photos. For a nightlife perspective of downtown, head to the swanky hotel development, Metropolitan at the 9, and look out from the Azure Lounge to see Playhouse Square and more dazzling landmarks. Whether you're looking for a farm-to-table meal, craft cocktail, or just hoping to soak up the atmosphere of East 4th, the Greenhouse Tavern offers the only rooftop dining in the city.

Tower City Observation Deck, 230 W Huron Rd., Cleveland
216-623-4750, towercitycenter.com

Azure Lounge, 2017 E 9th St., Cleveland
216-239-1200, azure9cle.com

Greenhouse Tavern, 2038 E 4th St., Cleveland
216-443-0511, thegreenhousetavern.com

HAVE A SIMPLY
WONDERFUL, QUIRKY HOLIDAY

In Cleveland, we embrace our cold-weather holidays. And as the snow blankets the city, we still shovel our walkways (another local rite of passage) and celebrate our most off-beat Christmas traditions. Make like Ralphie and check out A Christmas Story House in Tremont where parts of the beloved movie were shot. Just look for the leg lamp in the window. Medina is home to Hollywood Christmas Movieland, the world's largest privately owned collection of Christmas movie memorabilia. See Will Ferrell's costume from *Elf* and more at this emporium that brings the magic of the silver screen to Ohio. Kringle's Inventionasium is an off-the-wall, downright zany Christmas circus inside Tower City and is quickly becoming a winter tradition, even in all its absurdity. The Mad Hat green and purple interior and off-kilter characters make this an adventure in holiday oddities.

The very first industrial park in the world is also the most luminescent come nightfall. GE's Nela Park light display at GE Lighting Institute has glowed on for more than ninety years. Make it a Christmas Story day and visit the house followed by the performance in Cleveland's Playhouse Square district.

A Christmas Story House
1103 Rowley Ave., Cleveland
216-298-4919, achristmasstoryhouse.com

Hollywood Christmas Movieland
260 S Court St., Medina
330-721-6635, castlenoel.com

Kringle's Inventionasium
230 W Huron Rd., Cleveland
855-675-7464, mrkringle.com

GE's Nela Park Light Display
1975 Noble Rd., East Cleveland
gelighting.com

Cleveland Playhouse
A Christmas Story **Performance**
1501 Euclid Ave., Suite 200, Cleveland
216-241-6000, playhousesquare.org

WATCH THE STARS
AT MUELLER OBSERVATORY

One of the things rural dwellers say they'd miss if they lived in the city is looking up at the stars on a clear evening. Thanks to the Cleveland Museum of Natural History's Mueller Observatory, you can have the best of both worlds. Open on unclouded Wednesday nights, the observatory's ten-and-a-half-inch, motor-driven refracting telescope can be rotated 360 degrees. Thanks to a double shutter, greater sky exposure gives us a grander view into the great unknown. For budding amateur astronomers, the museum is also home to Shafran Planetarium. The design of the building allows nighttime visitors to use the building's angled roof to locate Polaris, the North Star. Regular Sky-Skan star shows take place in the titanium dome, where tour guides take you on a journey through space.

1 Wade Oval Dr., Cleveland
216-231-4600, cmnh.org

TIP

Expect large crowds at the Observatory
on nights of major sky events.

GET BUTTERFLIES
WITH THE BOTANICAL GARDENS AND MONARCH MIGRATION

The vibrant oasis of the Cleveland Botanical Gardens is home to themed, seasonal gardens, amazing playgrounds, and colorful events throughout the year. Your best bet is a tour with knowledgeable docents that can give you the backstory on each and every growth. Tours end in the steamy glasshouse, where the grand finale is a butterfly release.

If you notice an influx of densely packed butterfly photos shared amongst friends for a few days each year, it's because thousands of monarchs have landed in Cleveland en route to Mexico. The butterflies can be seen throughout the city, but many enthusiasts gather at Wendy Park, the only public park in the county that provides direct access to Lake Erie and the Cuyahoga River. The incredible clustering of monarchs comes every fall as they roost for the evening before continuing their journey.

Cleveland Botanical Gardens Butterfly Release
11030 East Blvd., Cleveland
216-721-1600, cbgarden.org

Wendy Park Monarch Migration
2800 Whiskey Island, Cleveland, 216-631-1800

TIP

Bring your cameras to the
Botanical Gardens. As the butterflies
burst free, plenty of the delicate creatures hang
around to land on the arms of observers.

RIDE
THE FAMOUS EUCLID BEACH CAROUSEL

It's striking enough to zoom through University Circle and see a spinning carousel that looks like it hasn't aged a day through the Western Reserve Historical Society's glass pavilion. But longtime Clevelanders will remember when the golden chariots spun in Euclid Beach Park, where they would take rides in the warm weather during family outings and field trips.

When the park closed in 1969, the classic carousel was shipped out of the city, and with it, the childhood memories of many. But resilient Clevelanders rarely let their beloved history slip from their fingers. With enough rallying and support, the ride was returned to its native home. Through extensive restoration, this delightful slice of Cleveland's past is back in motion like a time machine.

10825 East Blvd., Cleveland
216-721-5722, wrhs.org

FOLLOW THE TRACKS
TO THE MIDWEST RAILWAY
OPEN HOUSE

Few places are more distinctly Cleveland than the site of the Historic B&O Roundhouse in the Flats, one of the very few fully functional roundhouses in the country. Operated by the Midwest Railway Preservation Society, a volunteer-run organization that restores vintage cars and engines, the monthly open houses offer a glimpse into the history of how railroads played a major role in making Cleveland an industrial heavy hitter. The society would know a thing or two about that; they've been rescuing pieces of the past that would have otherwise been scrapped for a long time. You'll get to hop aboard the 1930s parlor coach "Mount Baxter," which was used in the Robert Redford flick *The Natural,* and tour guides will orate the history of the 4070 steam locomotive. Come prepared for plenty of stories from the past.

2800 W 3rd St., Cleveland
216-781-3629, midwestrailway.org

BE AWED
BY THE ART OF RESTORATION AT THE MUSEUM OF DIVINE STATUES

Artist Lou McClung recognized that churches were being decommissioned by the Cleveland Catholic Diocese. He also knew that there were priceless statues inside these buildings that someone had to rescue before the art was lost. At the Museum of Divine Statues in the former St. Hedwig's Church, McClung has been preserving the Catholic Church's history and traditional artwork. Within its walls, statues are returned to their original glory. Today, the more than one hundred statues lining the museum glow with more lifelike features and bolder, more authentic color. Modern touch-screen kiosks positioned throughout the museum provide photos and history of the statues. One need not be of any particular faith to revel in McClung's restoration work—a walk through this museum is a must for any art lover with a curiosity for peering into the past.

12905 Madison Ave., Lakewood
216-228-9950, museumofdivinestatues.com

EXPLORE THE LANDSCAPE
OF LAKE VIEW CEMETERY

Lake View Cemetery is one of Cleveland's most fascinating landmarks. Stroll through the sprawling 285 acres and you'll find stunning architecture and statuary such as the Haserot angel among the rolling hills. Look for signs of spring as the daffodil hill bursts into full bloom, along with other vivid horticulture. The towering tomb of President James A. Garfield is considered to be one of the country's first mausoleums. Wade Chapel is a visual wonder designed by Louis Comfort Tiffany and showcases a Tiffany stained glass window. On any given day, you'll see joggers, nature tours, and even weddings. And locals know to always leave a penny on the grave of Rockefeller for good luck. Of course, the land isn't just for sightseeing, it's a functioning graveyard that serves as the final resting place for many Cleveland notables.

2316 Euclid Ave., Cleveland
216-421-2665, lakeviewcemetery.com

SPEND THE NIGHT
AT FRANK LLOYD WRIGHT'S PENFIELD HOUSE

The Penfield House is one of only eight homes designed by the iconic architect Frank Lloyd Wright that welcomes overnight guests. Up to five people can stay in the elegant abode that defines Wright's modern approach to design. Surrounded by thirty wooded acres in Lake County with the Chagrin River running through the property, it's a tranquil respite that doesn't stray too far from city life. An overnight stay lets you experience Wright's design as it's meant to be—as if it's your own home. Built in the 1950s but bearing Wright's forward-thinking touch, the sleek interiors are a unique juxtaposition to the wilder outdoors. Don't be surprised to see deer grazing nearby and hear birds tweeting in the trees.

2203 River Rd., Willoughby Hills
penfieldhouse.com

CLIMB ON BOARD
THE CUYAHOGA VALLEY
SCENIC RAILROAD

This charming train ride cuts right through the Cuyahoga Valley National Park. An all-day pass means you can hop on and off the train as it winds through the park and stop at any attraction, which is a true testament to how many beautiful parts of the city are built around our natural surroundings. Dine at Crave along the Akron Northside Station, take in the sixty-seven-foot Brandywine Falls waterfall in Peninsula, and stop for a grilled cheese at the iconic Melt in Independence. Special excursions happen throughout the year, like the Grape Escape for wine lovers and Ales on Rails beer pairing. For little conductors, the annual Polar Express is a holiday wonderland for the whole family.

7900 Old Rockside Rd., Independence
330-439-5708, cvsr.com

STEP INSIDE
THE WORLD'S LARGEST GEODE, CRYSTAL CAVE

Hidden below Heineman's Winery on Put-In-Bay is the world's largest geode, Crystal Cave. The winery is worth a stop to on its own—it's Ohio's oldest family- owned and operated winery, dating back to 1888. In 1897, the geode was discovered while digging a well for Heineman's. Today, the winery offers tours through the cave by guides who pair the majestic views with history lessons. You'll pass a cascading waterfall along the way before heading into the earth, where shimmering Celestine crystals up to three feet long emerge around you. The staggering, incandescent surroundings are a reminder of the wonders that lie just below our feet.

978 Catawba Ave., Put-In-Bay
419-285-2811, heinemanswinery.com/crystalcave.asp

TIP

Wear comfortable shoes—you'll be hiking
up a steep path on your way back.

BE SAILORS FOR A DAY
AT THE STEAMSHIP *WILLIAM G. MATHER* AND USS *COD*

Along the waterfront are two capsules of historic nautical nostalgia. Stepping into the steely gray vessel of the USS *Cod* is like entering a time machine. As the last remaining World War II submarine still in its original condition, this national landmark is a piece of naval history. Pass through one end of the boat to the other while exploring compartments like the sleeping quarters, engine room, and control room.

The steamship *William G. Mather* is also known as "The Ship That Built Cleveland." Constructed in 1925, the ship transported cargo that helped bolster Cleveland as an industrial powerhouse. Explore all 618 feet including the cargo holds and pilot house, then climb onto the top deck for panoramic views of downtown.

USS *Cod*, 1089 E 9th St., Cleveland
216-566-8770, usscod.org

Steamship *William G. Mather*, Erieside Ave., Cleveland
greatscience.com/exhibits/steamship-william-g-mather.aspx

UNCOVER MARITIME MEMORIES
AT THE FAIRPORT HARBOR MARINE MUSEUM AND LIGHTHOUSE

The lighthouse of Fairport Harbor is the landmark of an area that was once called "Sailor's Town" for its prominence as a shipping port and for being one of the only stops along Lake Erie with a lighthouse. It's also remembered as being one of the final stops along the Underground Railroad. Inside the first Great Lakes lighthouse museum in the country, you'll find Coast Guard uniforms, models of freighters, and samples from the salt mines that exist two thousand feet below ground. Ascend the sixty-nine steps of the sixty-foot building to explore it all and stop on the observation deck for what feel like never-ending views of the lake. For those intrigued by the paranormal, legend says a ghost cat haunts the premises.

129 2nd St., Fairport Harbor
440-354-4825, fairportharborlighthouse.org

CRUISE
FOR CLASSIC CARS

With Cleveland's long automotive history, there's never a wrong time to celebrate classic cars, whether in a museum or outdoors on a hot summer day. At Canton Classic Car Museum, step into the vintage décor of this time capsule, where classic cars line the red carpets and a chandelier hangs overhead. Though it's a must-see for car lovers, there's more than just automobiles here. Movie posters and advertising, toys, and even political memorabilia are showcased throughout.

During the Lakewood Car Kulture Show, Madison Avenue is lined with hot rods, customs, bikes, scooters, and more while rock and roll and rockabilly bands play. It's a great excuse to stroll the streets, grab some Barrio tacos, and knock down pins at Madison-Square Lanes. Or try Willoughby Car Cruise-In where thousands gather every year as more than five hundred classic cars ride into the old-fashioned historic district of Downtown Willoughby.

Canton Classic Car Museum, 123 6th St SW, Canton
330-455-3603, cantonclassiccar.org

Lakewood Car Kulture Show
lakewoodcarkultureshow.com

Willoughby Car Cruise-In
willoughbyfrontierdays.com

CROSS
NORTHEAST OHIO'S BRIDGES

Cleveland is a city of bridges. Whether driving over them for a stunning view of the city or driving under them for a true-blue view of our industrial core, they tell the story of Cleveland in metal beams and cables. Explore the Detroit-Superior Bridge. Shrouded in mystery with its eerie acoustics, this unused streetcar-level bridge gives gorgeous views of the water below. Annual tours allow a peek into the otherwise closed-to-the-public territory.

Harness Cycle's Run the Bridges, hosted by the Hingetown spin studio, are a feet-to-the-pavement love letter to the Guardians of Transportation. Every month, runners come out in packs to beat their bridge-running personal records. For a cooldown? Cold-pressed juice at the neighboring Beet Jar Juice Bar.

Trek out to Ashtabula County for their Covered Bridge Tour. Visit Smolen-Gulf Bridge and Liberty Street Bridge, the longest and shortest covered bridges, respectively, in America.

Detroit-Superior Bridge, Cleveland
publicworks.cuyahogacounty.us

Harness Cycle's Run the Bridges, 2901 Detroit Ave., Cleveland
216-357-3258, harnesscycle.com

Ashtabula County's Covered Bridge Tour
25 W Jefferson St., Jefferson
440-576-3769, coveredbridgefestival.org

DROP BY
THE HILDEBRANDT
PROVISIONS COMPANY

Throughout our city, we see new life being breathed into old haunts. The Hildebrandt building dates back to its time as a meat processing company in the late 1800s. It's now a thriving home and incubator for small businesses.

Motorcycle fanatics can stop into Skidmark Garage, a vehicle repair operation dedicated solely to bikes. The popular artisan coffee roaster, Rising Star, planted its headquarters in its new warm, industrial space at Hildebrandt and has hosted everything from concerts to theater performances inside. For occasional events, the Hildebrandt Collective of eclectic artists will open up their studios to the public. Cleveland has always been about seeing new possibilities, and one walk through Hildebrandt's historic halls will cement the city's reputation for creativity.

3619 Walton Ave., Cleveland
216-961-9093, www.hildebrandtco.com

TIP
Annual open houses let you meet and greet all the small businesses that call the building home.

SHOPPING AND FASHION

CHANNEL YOUR INNER CHILD
AT VINTAGE TOY STORES

Spend a day getting back in touch with that sense of childlike wonder. Big Fun, a staple of Bohemian stomping ground Coventry Village, is brimming with off-the-wall throwback kitsch. Prepare for your senses to be overwhelmed while you dig through *Saved by the Bell* posters, gags and pranks, and old-school video games. A retro lover's paradise, you'll find everything from Ninja Turtles figurines to pop rocks. To truly make it old-school, stop in to its longstanding neighbor, Tommy's, for a burger (or veggie burger) and a shake.

Nostalgia reigns supreme in the Waterloo Arts District, but never as playfully as at Star Pop Vintage and Modern. Classic action figurines, novelty lunchboxes, and trinkets of yesteryear mingle on the shelves. Plus, you'll find plenty of vintage t-shirts and vinyl records to rummage through.

Big Fun, 1814 Coventry Rd., Cleveland Heights
216-371-4386, bigfuntoystore.com

Star Pop Vintage and Modern, 15813 Waterloo Rd., Cleveland
216-965-2368, starpopcleveland.com

DIVE
INTO COMICS, ZINES, AND SMALL PRESS BOOKS

Cleveland has a rich history in the small press world, from the archives of d.a. levy to our wealth of indie bookstores. Even behind the scenes of the Rock & Roll Hall of Fame's Library and Archives, *Rolling Stone* magazines intermingle with *Riot Grrrl* zines. Check out Genghis Con Cleveland. This small press convention helmed by John G., the artist behind Melt's artwork and the *Lake Erie Monster* comic series, brings together the best in indie comics and zines. A longstanding bookstore in Bohemian hub Coventry Village, Mac's Backs hosts readings and discussions in its basement. Part new and part used bookstore, part zine archive and part small press, Guide to Kulchur has published some of the most exciting and challenging works in the city, including its own quarterly. Everything from poetry readings to hip-hop sets to theater productions have taken place between their walls.

Genghis Con Cleveland
genghisconcleveland.blogspot.com

Mac's Backs, 1820 Coventry Rd., Cleveland Heights,
216-321-2665, macsbacks.com

Guide to Kulchur, 5900 Detroit Ave., Cleveland
216-314-4644, guidetokulchurcleveland.com

SHOP THE ANTIQUE DISTRICTS
OF LORAIN AVENUE AND LARCHMERE BOULEVARD

Everyone loves finding a piece of the past. These sellers take memorabilia from Cleveland's gritty past and don't clean them up too much—just enough. The Lorain Avenue Antiques District, with enough concentrated shops to weave easily from one to another, is every vintage lover's first stop. Find housewares at Century Antiques and old paintings and curiosities at Nook n Cranny, give things a second life with Reincarnation Vintage Design, and visit Cleveland's ultimate emporium of oddities, Sweet Lorain.

Travel to the quaint neighborhood of Larchmere, where antique shops are interspersed between little cafes and complement a number of art and décor stores. Stop into Elegant Extras to add just the right touches of porcelain and crystal, visit The House Warmings for furniture, and Marc Goodman's Antique Mall for a mish-mash of vendors. From retro kitsch to mod to rustic, there's a bit of every kind of treasure in these neighborhoods.

Century Antiques
7410 Lorain Ave., Cleveland, 216-281-9145
centuryantiquescleveland.com

Nook n Cranny
5201 Lorain Ave., Cleveland, 216-281-6665

Reincarnation Vintage Design
7810 Lorain Ave., Cleveland, 216-651-9806
rvdcleveland.com

Sweet Lorain
7105 Lorain Rd., Cleveland, 216-281-1959
sweetlorain.com

Elegant Extras
12900 Larchmere Blvd., Cleveland, 216-791-3017

The House Warmings
3001 Larchmere Rd., Shaker Heights, 216-618-1060

Marc Goodman's Antique Mall
12721 Larchmere Blvd., Cleveland, 216-229-8919

More:
larchmere.com
discoverlorainave.com

TAKE A DAY TRIP
TO CHAGRIN FALLS

The pretty-as-a-peach Chagrin Falls whisks you away to another era with its quaint downtown and roaring waterfall. It's notably also the hometown of *Calvin and Hobbes* creator Bill Watterson, and it is largely speculated that he based much of the look of his beloved cartoon strip on these suburban Ohio surroundings. Warm as the name implies, Fireside Book Shop is a neighborhood independent bookstore with three floors of best-sellers and used treasures.

Sugary sweet in both treats and old-fashioned charm, the Chagrin Falls Popcorn Shop serves up popcorn, candy, and ice cream, and has been around since 1949. Just look for the iconic red, white, and blue awning and follow the aroma of summertime confections.

At Dave's Cosmic Subs, fresh subs slathered in delicious Dave's Cosmic Sauce all started here. The groovy sandwich shops with tie-dyed walls full of rock memorabilia are now found all over the country. Setting the stage since the 1930s, Chagrin Valley Little Theatre is one of the nation's oldest community theaters. Spend a night out at the theater watching locals steal the show.

Fireside Book Shop
29 N Franklin St., Chagrin Falls
440-247-4050, firesidebookshop.com

Chagrin Falls Popcorn Shop
53 N Main St., Chagrin Falls
440-247-6577, chagrinfallspopcorn.com

Dave's Cosmic Subs
9 River St., Chagrin Falls, 440-247-9117
https://www.davescosmicsubs.com

Chagrin Valley Little Theatre
40 River St., Chagrin Falls
440-247-8955, cvlt.org

FIND VINYL
AT SPECIALTY RECORD SHOPS

Record stores can tell you a lot about a city, which is why they should be some of the first stops in the rock 'n roll capital of the world. More than that, Cleveland has a bevy of indie shops, each with its very own specialty.

Heavier rockers need not go farther than the expansive My Mind's Eye. For all things funk, soul, hip-hop, and R&B, stop into Young Kings, Nikki's Music, and Calhoun Record Shop. Visit Bent Crayon or Hanson Records for all things experimental and electronic. Punk and new-wave listeners have long patronized Hausfrau Record Shop for all their needs. LOOP can satisfy your cravings for a cup of joe and funky shoes along with indie favorites. Record Revolution is a Coventry Village staple. Square Records and Hollow Bone Records add to the Akron scene. And every record store browsing day begins at Record Den—enough said.

My Mind's Eye
16010 Detroit Ave., Lakewood, 216-521-6660
mymindseye.com

Young Kings
1418 W 29th St., Cleveland, 216-644-1058

Nikki's Music
11701 Buckeye Rd., Cleveland, 216-991-0011
nikkismusic.com

Calhoun Record Shop
356 Reed Ave., Akron, 330-212-5334

Bent Crayon
1305 W 80th St., Cleveland, 216-221-9200
bentcrayonrecords.com

Hanson Records
25 1/2 W College St., Oberlin, 440-985-8263
hansonrecords.bigcartel.com

Hausfrau Record Shop
1388 W 65th St., Cleveland, 216-394-5171

Loop Coffee
2180 W 11th St., Cleveland, OH 44113

Record Revolution
1832 Coventry Rd., Cleveland Heights, 216-321-7661

Square Records
824 W Market St., Akron, 330-375-9244
squarerecordsakron.com

Hollow Bone Records
2721 W Market St., Fairlawn, 330-285-3232
hollowbonerecords.com

Record Den
7661 Mentor Ave., Mentor, 440-946-9909

SHOP
THE 5TH STREET ARCADES

Duck into this eclectic indoor mall in the heart of downtown. Filled with retail, food, and art galleries, sunshine pours through the airy skylight as you shop. Whimsical paper flowers create colorful bouquets at Love, Anji, and all the ingredients for mixing up craft cocktails can be found at Happy Hour Collection. Find treats for your furry friend at CLE Pets or pick up a dapper accessory at The Whatknot Bow Tie Company. Of course, there is more than trinkets and treasures here. Grab a cup of fresh-brewed coffee at Pour Cleveland, fill up on sausages at Picnic, and satisfy your sweet tooth at Colossal Cupcakes. It's also home to beloved local chains. Get your brunch on with decadent breakfasts from Jack Flaps and build your own tacos at Barrio.

5th Street Arcades, 530 Euclid Ave., 216-583-0500, 5thstreetarcades.com

Love, Anji, 216-282-4076, loveanji.com

Happy Hour Collection, 216-563-1166, happyhourcle.com

The Whatknot Bow Tie Company, thewhatknot.com

Pour Cleveland, 216-479-0395, pourcleveland.com

Picnic, 216-804-5550, picnic-cle.com

Colossal Cupcakes, 216-938-9609, colossalcupcakes.com

Jack Flaps Luncheonette, 216-961-5199, jack-flaps.com

Barrio, 216-862-4652, barrio-tacos.com

SUGGESTED
ITINERARIES

SURF & TURF

PAMPER YOUR PALATE

OUTDOOR ADVENTURES

CULTURAL AFFAIR

THE QUIRKY PATH

DATE NIGHT

FUN FOR THE FAMILY

ACTIVITIES
BY SEASON

SPRING

Cleveland International Film Festival – March/April, 54

Lottery League – April, 72

St. Patrick's Day Parade – March, 57

Hessler Street Fair – May, 62

SUMMER

Twins Days – August, 64

Summer Solstice – June, 51

Studio-A-Rama, 58

Wade Oval Wednesday, 30

FALL

Monarch Migration, 110

Woollybear Festival, 53

Ingenuity Fest, 52, 58

WINTER

INDEX